Management and Ministry
– appreciating contemporary issues

EDITOR'S NOTE

MODEM is a new national organisation. It has been formed to promote the relevance of sound management to the churches and the mutuality of interest between churches and secular organisations.

This is MODEM's first publication. It aims to set the agenda for management/ministry issues in the 1990s. Based on an overview provided by Archdeacon Malcolm Grundy, I invited a panel of recognised authorities drawn mainly from MODEM members to address these issues. Their brief was to open them up for serious debate by church leaders and church users, and everyone who supports MODEM's aim of promoting the mutuality of interest and hence dialogue between the churches and secular organisations.

JOHN NELSON
1 May 1996

ACKNOWLEDGEMENTS

In editing and collating material from many sources I first wish to record my sincere thanks to all the contributors for their helpful cooperation. Secondly I wish to thank the Venerable Malcolm Grundy who has been my Editorial Adviser throughout the preparation and compilation of this volume. Thirdly I wish to express my thanks to Kenneth Baker and The Canterbury Press Norwich for carefully seeing the work through publication.

J.N.

FOREWORD
by
Sir John Harvey-Jones, MBE

I am delighted to have been asked to write the foreword for this book. The need for better management is ubiquitous. Churches need to be well managed, perhaps even more than private sector profit-seeking organisations do. Unfortunately, the need for the churches' work will always far exceed the money available. All the more reason therefore for the highest standards of management to ensure that the resources available are put to the most appropriate use. At the same time, business leaders do not have a monopoly of experience, or of management skills. MODEM is just the sort of organisation that I would have dreamt of being set up. It aims not only to promote the relevance and application of good management practice to the churches, but also to encourage the links between the churches and secular organisations. This book will, I hope, be read by people in business and by those who are interested in the theory and practice of management, and by everyone of us who uses the facilities offered by churches of every denomination.

CONTENTS

Editor's Note   *page* iii

Foreword by Sir John Harvey-Jones, MBE   v

Overview by Malcolm Grundy, Archdeacon of Craven   3

PART ONE: **AGENDA FOR MINISTRY**
1. Inherited concepts of leadership   31
2. Pastoral theology re-defined   37
3. Affirming lay ministries   59
4. Reclaiming vocation for the whole people
   of God   67
5. Relationships in mixed gender parishes   73
6. Developing a reflective spirituality in
   management   83
7. Towards redefining the role of ministry   91
8. Understanding new patterns of management
   in ministry   99

PART TWO: **AGENDA FOR ORGANISATION**
9. The church as a voluntary man-profit
   organisation   111
10. How to revive the Church   119
11. Get up and go!   125
12. Churches as places of learning   133
13. Quality ministry   141
14. Quality at work   147
15. Appropriate professional support and
    development   155
16. Asking 'Why' questions now   171
17. Appraisal schemes   177
18. Human resource management   187
19. Information Technology in church mission
    and strategy   201

MODEM's *background*   221

Contributors   227

Short Bibliography   231

Index   235

OVERVIEW

Overview

MALCOLM GRUNDY

MANAGEMENT WITHIN THE CHURCHES

Mention the word management within some church groups and an immediate hostility is likely to emerge. Reasons for this are deep-seated. Feelings and emotions are touched bringing reminders of bad experiences. Management is about impersonal systems bringing a cruel efficiency to an organisation with little concern for the lives of those involved. Management is decision making dictated by the balance sheet. Management is about authority and power when the Gospel is about the one who became powerless. Management conjures up a whole range of concepts which contrast with the human, person-centred message of the Christian Gospel.

There is an awareness developing that new ways are needed to organise our churches. The concern of MODEM is that church and secular learn from one another. Can good management possibly be compatible with the informal, voluntary, nature of our congregations where people give so generously of their time and energy? Is management an appropriate concept for the inspired amateurism which has been so much a characteristic of the life of our churches and our clergy? Some of the most able clergy in large parishes have been outstanding managers. Very many clergy would not see their primary task to be that of a manager.

This introductory chapter will point to key areas in the life of the churches where implicit understandings of management are already being practised. It will look at some of the changes which are taking place in church and society and will point to places where the management of change is a

3

pressing need. There will also be a re-examination of some of the historic understandings of management which have come to us from the Bible and from church tradition. There will be a concluding range of suggestions which can form an agenda for the debate about the appropriate practice of management by anyone who holds a position of responsibility in local congregation or national church.

Those who take on responsibilities within our churches experience rapid change accompanied all too often by severe financial constraints. No one should be left unsupported, to sink or swim by using their wits and experience alone. One of the worst features of our church life has been the emergence of a win-lose, praise-blame culture. Effective and well understood management practices are pastoral. They ensure that adequate training and support are given. Good practice learns from mistakes and builds on challenge and opportunity.

When we take on responsibilities in our church we often have our own view or 'model' of the good practitioner we want to be. Sometimes this has a Biblical or theological basis, sometimes it is the reflection of someone who has influenced us in the past. Each of us wants to be a worthy servant of God. We stand in an overwhelming tradition of prophets, priests, pastors and saints who have gone before us. Our roots are in the traditions which they have created. But we do not stand where they stood. These are new and different times. We are called, as the Anglican service for the induction of a new minister says, 'to proclaim the faith anew in each generation'. Effective management will assist that proclamation. It will have a regard for the individual and for the church. That care will often be expressed in a long-term view which sometimes means that hard decisions have to be taken. Effective management provides the tools for church leaders to tackle head-on the challenges which face us as we try to live Christian lives which are both humble and wise.

'My own battle scars'

To try to develop good management practices within the

churches is to be marked by the scars of battle. Let me describe three which have marked me. On one unforgettable occasion in the Diocese of London when my clergy training colleague and I were attempting to suggest that some forms of in-service training might be of a little help, one enormous and redfaced clergyman attacked us, 'My great grandfather was a chaplain at the battle of Waterloo, how dare anyone suggest to me how I might do my job'! Tradition and a sense of continuity are both a help and a hindrance in looking at management within the churches. 'We have always done it this way' and 'What did we do last time' are the response of those who have refined their approach and stand in a long tradition of service. They are also the approaches of arrogance, complacency and conservatism – of organisations in decline. More than anything else clergy learn from colleagues they admire. Some base their whole ministries on sayings of their college principal or their first vicar, though not many are actually practising the skills of getting alongside people learned by chaplains in the wars of this century – or even at Waterloo. Clergy learn most by doing, whether they admit it or not, by on the job training and by reflecting on that experience.

A second of my scars is an early experience of getting clergy to discuss the management of their time. The lessons learned remain with me to this day. As an Industrial Chaplain in Rotherham I arranged for the Training Manager of a major private steel company to talk about the management of time to a group of local clergy. He was outstandingly good, clear and simple. Of course he talked about giving priorities to work, about managing a diary, about analysing work over a week and a month, about comfortable roles and uncomfortable roles and much more. Questions after were interesting and relevant. Then one of our number said he could not go along with the general drift. His days had to be open, unplanned, as did his weeks, he needed to be open and available to the Holy Spirit's guidance and promptings at any time. Many of the rest of us were embarrassed. I felt like falling through the floor. Our Training Manager, calm and very firm said 'Well there may be 5% of your day or week where the spirit holds you. I cannot help you there. For the rest you will be using skills much the same as anyone else. With training and improved management skills I can help you to do them better.'

My third scar in trying to develop management skills among clergy comes from their often repeated understanding of their persona. A priest or vicar or minister is not to be described as having a job. It is a calling or vocation in that particular sense of the word. It is for life, no hours of work can be set, no restrictions can be placed on what should be done. The emphasis, in a phrase from the sixties, is on being rather than doing. This understanding of ministerial priesthood is reflected in how the clergy are paid. Roman Catholic priests can hardly be said to be paid at all. They are 'kept', in allowances, in kind and in accommodation, for life. In return they accept the considerable restrictions on personal freedom which this entails. Anglican clergy are not paid a salary, they receive a 'stipend' which frees them to develop their ministries. They are housed in tied accommodation and consequently find it very difficult to move in and out of stipendiary ministry. Security is almost certain until retirement which comes with a lump sum and a non-contributory pension. Free-Church ministers generally receive a lower annual amount than Anglicans, but the allowances they receive make the stated annual figure irrelevant to the actual amount spent on their keep. It is the Salvation Army where Officers come closest to having to earn their own keep. Payment by results is very close to home for their local staff and is similar in Baptist and Pentecostal Churches.

The three areas of objection to the concepts of management by ministers I have described go some way to explain the depth of resistance. To them may be added the fact that some will have come to ordination after a bad experience of managing or being managed. In an often unexpressed way they see the church as a 'safe haven'. The Principal of Ridley Hall in Cambridge where the 'God on Monday' project was launched for ordinands said it was impossible to get many of them to reflect on their work experience for at least one year after they had entered college. Management and all that goes with it was something they had left behind.

These objections have some substance to them and are not

to be dismissed lightly. They are to be recognised as the real framework for ministry of large numbers of clergy in each of our major denominations. They also reflect the training and learning culture of our churches. The first cultural objection is that the role is inherited, its traditions passed on, as if by osmosis, as entrants begin their life in the new role. The second spiritual objection is that God guides and directs a minister's life. The church occasionally speaks or acts giving guidance but there is maximum scope for individualism to flourish. The third objection is expressed financially. Clergy are not paid to do a job. They are sustained in order to live out a role as 'holy persons'.

THE SCIENCE OF MANAGEMENT

Some key terms

If management is to be taken seriously then it has to be treated as a discipline. This requires analysis and application. Analysis of the current understandings by church leaders of the use of words describing their own understanding of their work is a good place to start. There is a difference between leadership and management.[1] This will be introduced after these descriptions and may help to clarify the range of under-standings within key words and concepts. We are exploring here questions of ecclesiology, about what our churches are, what they are for and how they work, the application of our theology to our practice.

Shepherd

One very widely used image favoured by church leaders of many denominations is that of shepherd. It has its origins in the life of King David who began his working life as a shep-herd and rose, through God's election, and the use of skills he had learned, to be a wise and powerful king. The prophet Isaiah uses the images of sheep in key passages. Jesus used some of these to identify himself with the suffering and sacri-fice needed to atone for a people's sins. With an extension of the metaphor it was the shepherd who gave his life for his sheep. This image was taken up most strongly by St John in his re-timing of the last days of Jesus' life so that his death was understood as sacrifice. More directly in one of his 'I am' passages St John describes Jesus as the 'Good Shepherd'.

This range of understandings of Shepherd – Sheep in the Hebrew and Christian scriptures – is taken up in the language and understandings of the good Bishop, priest and minister. The Good Shepherd knows the sheep and is known by them. The lost sheep is searched for and found amid much rejoicing. The sheep will follow the shepherd whom they know and whose voice they recognise. The true shepherd stays with the flock when danger is near and does not run away like the hired watchman.

So also the Good Shepherd, Bishop, President, Chairman, Moderator, will be the focus of unity amid those under his or her charge. They will try to hold together different factions and groups within the flock and only rarely will they take sides themselves. They will defend their traditions but will also lead the flock on to new and more nourishing pastures when the old ones cease to provide adequate food. The Good Shepherd is always available and always has time for those in need. The Bishop carries the pastoral staff – a shepherd's crook as the symbol of this understanding of the office. The good secular manager works in a similar way, perhaps with a greater freedom to take decisions when consensus is not working, but the shepherd image is little used outside church circles.

Bridge Builder

As a young student at King's College, London I was one of a group invited to attend the service in Westminster Cathedral when Cardinal Heenan was welcomed. He spoke of one of the titles of his office, Pontifex Maximus, and chose to interpret it as 'Bridge Builder'.

The opportunity which church leaders have to span different groups in society is enormous, far more than the relative size of their denomination or congregation would merit. The good leader will use and manage these opportunities to great advantage and will be at ease when moving between groups as part of the work. Increasingly, for church leaders, this is a management skill which has to be learned. It is certainly a skill which is expected of the good Bishop, Moderator, Chairman, local priest or minister. As our society has changed, so the social background of local and natural leaders has become much more diverse. There is a role for the skilled church leader in bringing together people and groups who find it difficult to understand one another.

Church leaders are bridge builders and as such exercise a leadership role in society which is not part of their internal, ecclesiastical job but is one which no other leader in society has a similar opportunity to develop. When leaders see their work primarily as within their own denomination they do not see the half of the job opportunities open to them.

The Curé d'Ars

The role of personal management overwhelmingly preferred by lay people is that of the good pastor. The priest, vicar or minister earning the highest points from those inside and outside the church is the one who visits people in their homes, who can give helpful personal and spiritual advice and who can listen. This same model is the one held by many clergy as the activity which is 'really their job'. In lists of activities carried out in the week, those requiring administration are frequently rated as very low and those where people are met face-to-face rated highest. Depending on the emphasis of the tradition the roles of celebrant of the eucharist and of pastor and friend are those which fit best the understanding of the 'priestly' office. The Curé d'Ars was a French village priest to whom people came for advice and to make their confession and who became a model for good priestly ministry.

Leadership and selection

To be a leader, to engage in community activity, to be a good administrator, preacher or prophet requires great ability with interpersonal skills.

If such a high value is given to the skills of ministry a number of things appear as strange in the conduct of contemporary clergy. Not least is the fact that so many lack any evident ability to relate well to other people as individuals or in large groups. Many are particularly ill at ease in small groups and in handling meetings.

Part of the reason for this is that criteria for selection do not appear to relate to the role and skills which are required to undertake ministerial tasks. Another serious reason for the non-development of latent skills appears to be the effect which ecclesiastical structures have on the behaviour of otherwise relatively 'normal people'. I shall return to both of these aspects of dysfunctional behaviour in later observations.

What really has to be examined is the basic *Curé d'Ars* concept of the place of clergy within their congregations in the next decade. I do not want to suggest that clergy should or should not fit these roles. What has to be established is the range of tasks which need to be undertaken and managed within a local congregation, what are the 'core' tasks which clergy need to undertake themselves, whatever their natural temperament, which tasks they can negotiate for themselves, and which tasks will be undertaken by others in the local congregation, who may well need both special training and also to know that they are supported and encouraged in the work by their priest or minister. How can clergy learn to work collaboratively and inspire others by their example in enabling a participative style to characterise their churches?

Leadership and Management

Leading the work of a local church is different from managing it. Thomas.P. Sweester in an article in the Jesuit Journal *Human Development*, Autumn 1993, develops this difference and begins with an example from the ministry of Jesus.[1]

'Take a look at Jesus and his followers. That was a leadership interaction. Not only did Jesus influence the people, but they influenced him as well ... Both Jesus and the people intended real changes. These changes were not always the same or well articulated, but they were genuinely desired. Jesus brought a breath of fresh air, a new authority. The people longed for freedom, for less oppression, for a better way of life. Jesus offered a way out of routine and boredom. Jesus' purposes and those of the people were in harmony.'

So much for leadership. What about management? According to one definition, 'Management is an authority relationship between at least one manager and one subordinate who co-ordinate their activities. This is not leadership. It does not include the notion of change. Instead the focus is on getting a task done. There is an interaction which takes place between a manager and a subordinate, but it does not have the same mutuality as leadership. Someone is in charge to see that a task is accomplished. Others help to get that task done.' We are dealing with situations where a mixture of leadership and management is required.

There is a great wealth of experience and there are now libraries of books about management. The emergence of organisations like MODEM shows now that there is also a tremendous willingness for experience to be shared. There are similarities between managing commercial organisations and charitable, voluntary, agencies like churches. One of the primary harmonising concepts is that of the 'Learning Organisation', a place where ideas can be received and shared and where leadership flows from a highly motivated and energised group of people.

MODERN MANIFESTATIONS OF MANAGEMENT

Over the past twenty years or more there have developed assumptions about new styles of leadership and management which are required in the churches. These often contrast with the three main traditional understandings which I have just described. To some these newer ways are not innovative at all and are the continuation of a style which they would say their denomination has always fostered, or even stood for. To very many others these new ways of working have sat unhappily with their concept of the ordained ministry. This unease has been fostered by an ecclesiastical culture which implicitly encourages individualism – not to say eccentricity.

New demands on ministry

The multiple charge appointment

All mainstream denominations have experienced a decline in

the number of those available for full-time, paid work. At the same time, because congregations have reduced and populations have moved, it has seemed right to join parishes or congregations together under the charge of one or more minister. In some rural areas one Anglican vicar may have four or five churches. In many urban, inner city areas clergy may have two congregations. Much the same is true for Roman Catholic priests, though the need to work participatively has come to them a little later, Documents of Vatican II notwithstanding. Methodist ministers have always had groups of churches in Circuits and work within a system of lay responsibility for buildings and pastoral care which was born with Methodism itself.

It is the priest or minister who has the pastoral, *Curé d'Ars*, model for approaching the work who has the most difficulty with the multiple congregation charge. The most conscientious will be overworked in trying to be the confidant of people in communities which are quite separate. The range of meetings, services and organisations can overwhelm. Coincidence of timing of events alone can make it impossible for even the expected appearances to be made. A sense of guilt can be induced, if not one of failure. The only person experiencing more pressure and meetings is perhaps the minister from either denomination who has accepted a joint URC/Methodist responsibility.

These situations ask for local responsibility to be given to members of congregations. The minister who has difficulty in even sharing out basic work which the sole charge person may be able to'carry out will come into conflict with those on the ground who try to fill the vacuum. Head-on clashes are likely to result. A failure to communicate is probable. Able lay people will give up and allow the minister to take too much on. Congregations almost certainly decline as a result.

A new kind of management skill is required in these situations. Co-ordination and delegation are essential. The skills of good organisation can be very pastoral. If the minister really cannot organise, then an administrator or secretary can take this on. Lay people need to be trained, informed, trusted and equipped for their new responsibilities. One of the most important tasks of the minister is to be able to support the lay visitors, managers and organisers in their work. The minister with a multiple charge needs to be trained and supported by those in senior positions in the denominations.

A theology of the laity

Not since Reformation times has there been such a widespread belief that the ministries of lay people should have such importance. This is true both of understandings of ministries in the world and in the church. The history of this re-awakening is fascinating but cannot even be sketched out here. The Parish and People Movement of the 1950s and 1960s was certainly a major attitude changing influence.

Wherever the emphasis is placed, by the 1960s important theological reconstructions of the ministries and priesthood of the laity were under way. Herald of the 'New Reformation' – the title of one of his books – was Bishop John Robinson who edited a collection of influential essays called *Laymans Church*.[2] More important for many lay discussion groups was *God's Frozen People* by Mark Gibbs and Ralph Morton.[3] That title's description of Christian laity said it all for very many people. At the same time the Second Vatican Council produced revolutionary documents about an enhanced place for the laity in the Roman Catholic Church. In England and Wales this was followed by a liberating Lay Eucharistic Congress in Liverpool in 1980 called 'The Easter People'. The volcanic lava of enthusiasm which these publications and events engendered has subsided somewhat now as old clerical models have re-asserted themselves and disillusionment has set in. However, they have left an indelible mark in church structures and have affected the management of congregations in ways which allow no going back.

Adult learning

One of the most significant contributions the churches have made to education in the last half-century is the development and practice of theories about how adults learn. In Britain this understanding has been pioneered by adult education officers working ecumenically but initially focussed around the Church of England Board of Education.[4] The contribution is particularly in the field of experiential education. Business schools and industrial trainers have made equally important contributions to skills training and organisational analysis. The writing and analysis of Peter Rudge brought this thinking to some church people.

One of the most important discoveries is that people learn in different ways at different stages in their lives and that adults learn, and change their behaviour, by bringing their life experience into action. New knowledge is set against life experience. Most learning is done through action and by reflection upon activity. Parents learn by setting up a Playgroup. Campaigners learn through getting involved in bringing about change. Their performance becomes more effective as they reflect on their activities and learn from them. The British pioneering work was influenced by Latin American activists and particularly by Paulo Friere and his seminal work, 'The Pedagogy of the Oppressed'.[5]

Such discoveries were developed through 'experiental' participating workshops where trainers and course members were both part of the learning experience. These developments, widely used in theological education and in training within the denominations, encouraged and freed many lay people. No longer could the Vicar-led parish teaching occasions be regarded as acceptable. The Vicar, priest, or minister with special information ready to pour into eager empty learning vessels became increasingly isolated, a figure struggling against the tide of the way in which both adults and children were gaining their education and knowledge.[6]

Christian learners look to those who can transmit spiritual values, they want to dialogue with the priest and work alongside other enquirers where it is acceptable to say 'I don't know' and 'lets explore this together'. Journey has become an appropriate word for spiritual development and lifelong Christian learning.

Clergy using a hierarchical, pyramidal, method of managing their congregations find dialogue difficult. They attract laity who prefer dependence and the security of being told what to do. Such Christian communities sometimes appear to flourish but frustration and the lack of freedom eventually drive out those who want to continue to grow. The insecurity of British life in the 1980s and 90s has led many to join 'fundamentalist' churches offering just these certainties. Such Christian encounters may be right for some searchers and new believers. There is an important managerial training task to be done with ministers of these churches who see faith being 'watered down' as people grow and ask questions. With the strength of evangelical groupings within the denominations, managing growth and development will be a key task for the next decade. 'Church Plants', the establishment of congregations divided off from their parent church, require particular management skills at the local and at the denominational level.

TODAY'S ORGANISATIONAL ISSUES

It is now time to begin to focus on questions of management in the churches which arise as a consequence of the considerable changes which have taken place over these last thirty years. I will outline key issues which set the agenda for the next decade. Others will then develop these agenda issues in a series of contributions which make up the rest of the book.

Teams and groups

After at least thirty years of Team and Group Ministries in the Church of England no authoritative way has yet been found to manage these multiple congregation, multiple staff arrangements. There are a number of reasons for this. Many Teams and Groups have not developed from a long-term piece of local co-operation but have had arbitrary boundaries imposed upon them which may look good on paper but which do not work on the ground. Finances have had to be put into a common fund. The concept is right and just but if trust and goodwill have not been established then only rivalry can result. Clergy have grown up with the individualistic model of their own ministries. They have not yet been able to learn or maintain the kind of Team commitment which requires negotiation and allegiance to group decisions.

There are exceptions to all these statements but the horror stories from so many pieces of work give them a weight which cannot be ignored. Linked with the lack of shared experience about Teams and Groups comes the confusion which surrounds the picture of the concepts of shared or collaborative ministry.

Collaborative Ministry

If collaboration means taking others into an open and honest partnership where people and groups co-operate, share strengths and weaknesses, and work towards a common good, then few congregations can say they have approached success. All too often, in spite of countless worthy remarks, collaborative ministry can mean no more than sharing out the pool of tasks which have to be done among a wider group of people. Even worse it can mean sharing out the Vicar's or Priest's jobs among the *same* group of people in a congregation.

Unless the theology of ministry is approached at the same time, shared ministry is a drudgery. People will only commit themselves to new tasks if they can be excited by the prospect of what they are contributing. Equally, clergy will only become confused and insecure if they see some of their traditional tasks being taken away and no newly negotiated concept of their contributions put in its place. A vacuum of leadership can develop when an absence of authority and accountability emerges and, at best, management is by committees. This iş a travesty of shared ministry. New management techniques are demanded, not no management.

The Community Development Approach

Community development means that people and groups in a local situation learn how to work together as equals. It means that community workers and clergy do not initiate and lead local projects themselves. They are engaged in developing a framework where local people grow in confidence so that they can take increasing responsibility for local community initiatives.

Community Development skills can be of great value to

local ministers in work with their congregations. If they can become trained to enable others to take responsibility for work within the congregations then significant steps will have been taken towards the management skills required for collaborative ministry. In the deliberate use of the word 'process' to describe the experience of this method it is intended that participants will come to understand the theory, even the theology, implicit in this way of working. The pioneering work of Dr George Lovell on working non-directively has now become standard good community work practice. It is still less a characteristic of congregational life.[7]

NEW FEATURES REQUIRING MANAGERIAL ATTENTION

Two new features have become important in the lives of our churches which now need urgent managerial attention. These are, the employment of large numbers of lay people by the churches, and the failure of the restructuring of our ecumenical partnerships.

The employment of lay people

Dioceses and Districts which count up the number of lay people they employ find themselves with a surprising result. In addition to the number of lay officials and administrators, lay people are employed in considerable numbers in social or community projects. Money made available from funds for community work such as the Church Urban Fund and the Methodist Mission Alongside the Poor Programme have boosted funds and increased appointments. Unfortunately many grant funded appointments are short-term, often for three years. A surprising range of contractual agreements have been made and much dissatisfaction has resulted. The shortage of money within many denominations also means that lay posts are the first ones to be cut.

In management terms, denominations first need to recognise the responsibilities they have in employing lay people in such large numbers. Terms and conditions of employment, contracts and scales of pay need to be harmonised and in community projects more training needs to be given to those who are members of management committees. The new charity law legislation puts great responsibilities on those who are Trustees. Many in the churches who are involved in managing charitable money as Trustees of welfare projects require support and training to familiarise them with their new responsibilities.

A restructed ecumenism

The opportunity for ecumenical relationships to take a leap forward was offered in 1987 by the Swanwick Declaration in which the Roman Catholic Church in Britain declared itself willing to take a greater part as a full member. Cardinal Hume's speech on that occasion took many by surprise and was greeted with great enthusiasm.

An almost immediate restructuring took place with the British Council of Churches coming to an end and a new Council of Churches for Britain and Ireland (CCBI) being established in 1990. A new English body, 'Churches Together in England' (CTE) was established to complement organisations which existed in the other three nations. With the intending move from co-operation to commitment, local Councils of Churches were encouraged to become 'Churches Together'. Within England some 50 metropolitan/county Intermediate Bodies were also formed.

One of MODEM's early meetings was a seminar at Milton Keynes to hear an internal review of the working of some of the new structures. Already hinted at problems were brought to the surface. It is likely that the legalistic 'instruments' by which the new bodies were convened had a deadening effect on exciting possibilities. Responsibilities for leadership were not passed on to a new generation when appointments were made. Effective channels of communication from CCBI to local bodies hardly exist. Inertia and boredom appear to have set in. An exciting expansion of opportunities has been stifled, or so expert commentators say. Reasons for this appear to be primarily in the managerial decisions made at the outset. Those active in ecumenical agencies, often the most innovative areas of work, were not able to be full members in the new structures. A major organisational review is needed even at this early stage in the new work. There seems to be a reluctance to consider radical change. Fortunately, ecumenical activity at local level has not been affected by this inertia.

A NEW AGENDA

We have now reached a time when a new agenda has to be constructed for the development of the mainstream denominations over the next decade. Changes required are theological and require a re-appraisal of the philosophy of our organisations.

The new agenda has at its heart the need for responsible management within our churches. Such an acknowledgement is of a fundamental difference from any previous change. It is the nature of this change which will engage the authors of this book. A new science of the theologically resourced practice of management needs to be developed. This is a time of tremendous opportunity. Both experimentation and reflection are required. This needs to develop from the richness of our traditions. Our denominations are large and, by their very nature, can only change gradually as the attitudes and objectives of our members and staff are developed. Traditions are rich, they contain our histories and the answers to why we are as we are. Change within the churches has always had a personal, social, political and economic relationship to changes within the larger society. The threatened build walls to defend themselves. The secure build bridges of opportunity. Visionaries experiment with new structures. The suggestions which follow and the essays in the rest of this book offer those who are secure within their traditions and denominations, but who want them to continue to be vibrant, the opportunity to explore with us an agenda for the next ten years.

Bishop Leslie Hunter began his book *The seed and the fruit* with this story in 1939. It has long been an inspiration, and a comfort, to me.

> As the threats of war and the cries of dis-possessed were sounding in his ears, Western Man fell into an uneasy sleep. In

his sleep he dreamed that he entered the spacious store in which the gifts of God to man are kept, and addressed the angel behind the counter, saying: 'I have run out of the fruits of the Spirit. Can you restock me? When the angel seemed about to say no, he burst out, 'In place of war, afflictions, injustice, lying and lust, I need love, joy, peace, integrity, discipline. Without these I shall be lost'. And the angel behind the counter replied, 'We do not stock fruits, only seeds'.

A BUDGET OF OPPORTUNITIES

1.   Concepts of leadership

Today's good shepherd is not 'one man and his dog'. Today's sheep farmer is trained and experienced. Today's sheep breeders know how to get the very best from the herds and strains, the best for wool and the best for meat. Today's farmer knows about markets and prices, about competition, about living with risk and often an overdraft! The concept of the Good Shepherd as Bishop or leader needs developing to have a resonance with those who produce goods and manage people on the hills and dales of today's market economy.

Bridge builders can no longer be content with bringing people together and sitting down in complacency. They will find different groups in society can hardly communicate with one another. Bridge builders of today have to understand the concepts and presuppositions of groups in other religions and in our multi-value society. Bridge builders can analyse where people are coming from, interpret to others and, within it all, find a language through which spirituality can be transmitted.

The *Curé d'Ars* will discover a wider frame in which to be pastoral. This will include skills of helping the helpers and of ensuring a framework in which congregations can feel secure. The good pastor will develop a new inner security as a redefined role emerges. The employing denominations will move from a 'praise-blame' culture towards one which develops its employees, provides learning tools as roles are redefined and reinforces the work with its own spoken and unspoken values.

These analogies can be pressed further, others can be used from our traditions and perhaps new models tested as redefined and agreed roles emerge.

2. The selection of leaders

Ecclesiastical cultures foster and encourage individualism. Those who succeed in this 'Prima donna' world are promoted. Once in senior positions they are expected to work collaboratively. I do not think I overstate the situation too dramatically. Staff will not work at the theory and practice of collaborative ministry if they know that the actual route to recognition is by another way.

The selection of leaders within the denominations of course varies enormously but there are common threads. What is now required is a continuing review of the tasks required by leaders at different levels within the denominations and the development of ways of introducing potential leaders to the skills and responsibilities of the new work. It would be the fulfilment of a dream if an ecumenical staff college could be established to provide initial and inservice training for leaders at national, regional and local levels within the churches. It might well be a 'college without walls'.

3. Training in the discipline of management

If management is to be taken seriously within the churches then research needs to be financed to analyse precisely what the tasks are which need to be carried out, how structures work, how change can be managed, how conflict can be managed and discipline exercised.

Such a programme is not about the learning of skills alone – an activity based management – it is about developing a pastoral theology where a responsible practice of these tasks can be carried out. Such a need has become crucial for the Church of England as it begins to implement its 'Turnbull Report' on restructuring its central activities.[8]

4. Women and men

Churches are still predominantly managed by men. This will not be the case in ten years time. Already work is beginning on men and women working together as members of a parish staff and in teams. As more women become Team Rectors, Circuit Superintendants, District Chairmen, Moderators and, I am sure, Bishops, different approaches to the work will be discussed. Issues of sexuality within teams do affect the work. The masculine and feminine in each of us will become more definable as we learn to work together.

Unless a programme of learning from existing experience in the denominations, and from overseas, is begun there will be much heartache and misunderstanding. Men, women, wives, husbands and families will suffer and congregations will experience unnecessary hurt.

These new developments in ministry of men and women working together in leadership positions is already creating a new church. Let us find organisational ways of listening to the pioneers and learning from them.

The other side of learning in this situation is the management of divided churches. The sensitivity required to hold together staffs which contain those who are in favour of women's ordination and those who are against requires a charity which challenges honesty.[9]

5.   The learning organisation

This is a discipline which helps us develop an integrated system of management which allows not only continued learning but also the emergence of an organisation whose culture is one which is continually to be learning. Peter Senge[10] has described these as an integration of:

(a) Systems thinking – the knowledge that organisations and churches are fabrics of interrelated activities. Changes in one affects life in the others.

(b) Personal ministry – the discipline of continually clarifying and deepening our personal vision.

(c) Mental models – an understanding of the deeply held and ingrained assumptions, pictures, images, models, by which we view the world and which affect how we react and take action.

(d) Building a shared vision – the ability to mobilise people in an organisation or church around shared vision.

(e) Team learning – the ability of members and groups to 'dialogue together', suspend assumptions and enter into a genuine process of thinking together.

We shall need more research on churches as learning organisations.

6. Pulling out of decline

It is hard for church leaders not to feel that what they are actually managing is decline. As a consequence they have to carry overmuch criticism for their actions and their responsibilities are ones which receive little affirmation.

Management opportunities come with experiments to move aspects of a denomination out of decline into growth. The work of Martin F. Saarinen in an Alban Institute book on the life cycle of congregations here is helpful.[11] A beginning has been made in identifying and analysing characteristics of organisations/congregation from youthful adolescence – more energy than members, to maturity – join us and become like us, to decline – what did we do last time, to dying – do not invade my territory. Charles Handy has produced in *The empty raincoat*[12] his description of the Sigmoid Curve:

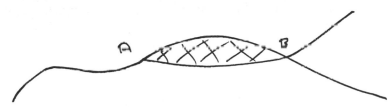

The area between A & B is a time when leaders, with an understanding of their task, can lift an organisation/denomination/church from decline to renewed vigour through experimental development of the tradition.

7. Review and Appraisal

A kind of appraisal system exists in almost every denomination. Enough information exists for a thorough critique to be carried out of systems in place and the implicit values which they carry.[13] Appraisal which is linked into hierarchical reviews might be strengthened if central Diocesan or District information data were shared. Clergy personal development and career development needs to be linked to the very important aspects of clerical life which must take regard of the partner's career and the needs of children to move schools in particular years.

Not enough work has yet been done on the benefits of peer-group appraisal. Where these schemes operate training and support need to be built in so that continuity can be ensured and interpersonal problems addressed.

8.   Standards of Quality

Not exactly a customers charter for every church, but it might be possible to suggest and describe the minimum standards which those who come into contact with a local church might expect. How long before phone calls or letters are answered, how frequently might the sick be visited by clergy and congregation members, could be basic examples.[14]

More systematically, attempts are now under way to analyse service and follow-up in local churches as a catalyst to higher quality contact with parishioners. The British Standard 5750 about quality assurance is being used as a springboard for this. Interesting first pieces of work have been done in the Diocese of Southwell and a bank of experience and analysis is beginning to accumulate.

9.   Wealth and Enterprise

Churches have an ambivalent attitude to the creation of wealth and the use of profits. One the one hand there is an awkwardness about handling money and the use of profits and on the other hand churches themselves cannot exist and cannot engage in charitable voluntary action without the results of wealth created by industrial and commercial practices.

There is a need to use the results of fifty years of industrial mission and to move beyond them. The everyday work which engages people needs to be capable of being offered up to God. The ethics of business and human relationships

within companies need continual re-examination. Within
congregations members need to be affirmed in their secular
work and supported in that rather than being valued only for
the contributions they make to church life.

10.   Escaping clericalism

We are in a phase which, in its present form, began with the
rise of the professions in the nineteenth century. It emphasises the skills of a priest set against the part played by lay
people in the church. This phase is likely to continue and to
be given new dimensions as women enter the priesthood in
larger numbers. They have to make their own different journey.

This new flowering will not be done at the expense of the
developing the responsibilities of lay people. It will be done
both alongside this lay movement and also in a complimen-
tary way to the adjustments which male priests will be
making in the new situation. Non-stipendary priests and
those entering the permanent Diaconate will also make their
mark.

These developments really will bring in a 'new Reformation' – but only if the base concept of Christian priesthood is
used as a starting point. The management of these moves
within churches is a vital area for analysis.

11.   Reflective practice in management

The central personal discipline for Christians as they manage
these changes will be 'reflective practice'. The understanding
of this core concept will be the key to renewed self-under-
standing and growth in organisational behaviour. Reflective
practice begins with understanding our experiences, moves
on to setting them alongside our Biblical traditions, explores
church teaching and then moves on to define new ways of
operating. It is spiritual direction, self and organisational
analysis, Biblical and doctrinal exploration all built into a
key accessible activity.[15]

12.   Managing in the market-place of values

Senior church leaders have a unique place in modern society.

Religious leaders, of any faith, will have enormous burdens and expectations placed upon them in the next ten years. Faiths and denominations need to be fully aware of what they are asking of those who come to this work and will need to provide appropriate professional support. No church leaders office and staff at the moment are adequate to support the demands which are being made. It will be one of the sadnesses of this decade if bridge-building and ecumenical management are abandoned through the pressures made by internal demands.

Good management requires able and intelligent leadership. The right kind of person will not be attracted unless the requirements of the work are clear. Whether the search is for a Circuit Superintendant or for an Archbishop, management and ministry need to be described, developed and supported in many ways never yet brought out into the open.

A BUDGET FROM THE PERSPECTIVE

The introductory, scene setting, parts of this chapter suggest topics already a part of our life which require development. Among them are:

> Collaborative Ministry
> Training for ministry to a mature laity
> Clergy Teams and groups
> Clergy Training for community development
> Management of the church as a voluntary non-profit organisation
> The management of ecumenism and ecumenical structures
> The development of a new science of the theologically resourced practice of management for the churches

When this challenge is understood our horizons will become broadened. Possibilities for a renewed, and quite different church can be explored by laity and clergy with a new kind of confidence about the future.

SPIRITUAL VALUES

It is possible in the 1990s to talk of spiritual values. They are openly used in secular organisations to describe both internal and customer relations. No longer must the associations of power, corruption and dirty hands be allowed to stay with Christian parodies of management. A marriage between spirituality and effective organisational practice can be a springboard for our society and not just for our religions if we can explore the new agenda being set and emerge with new understandings of what God is doing in a world which can never stand still and which will never be satisfied only by its past and its traditions.

NOTES

1. See, 'Parish Leadership Versus Parish Management', Thomas J. Sweester, *Human Development*, Autumn 1993.
2. John Robinson, *Layman's Church* (Lutterworth 1963).
3. M. Gibbs and T. Ralph Morton, *God's Frozen People* (S.C.M. 1961).
4. Described well by Yvonne Craig in *Learning for life* (Mowbrays, 1994).
5. Paulo Friere, *Pedagogy of the Oppressed* (Penguin, 1972).
6. See *Transforming Priesthood*, Robin Greenwood (S.P.C.K., 1995).
7. See *The Parchmore Partnership* (Lovell Rogers and Sharrocks, Chester House Publications, 1995).
8. *Working as One Body*, A report of the Archbishops' Commission on the organisation of the Church of England (Church House Publishing, 1995).
9. See articles on women and men in work relationships by Celia Hahn in *Action Information*, the Journal of the Alban Institute.
10. Peter Senge *The Fifth Discipline* (London Business Books, 1992).
11. Martin F. Saarinen 'The Life Cycle of a Congregation', Alban Institute, *Action Information*, May/June 1978.
12. Charles Handy *The Empty Raincoat* (Hutchinson, 1994).
13. David Jessett 'Towards a parishioner's charter? Quality in the Church.' *Ministry*, Summer 1993.
14. For details contact Dr Norman Todd, 39 Beacon Hill Road, Newark, Notts NG24 2JH.
15. See Malcolm Grundy *An Unholy Conspiracy* (TheCanterbury Press Norwich, 1992).

PART ONE

AGENDA FOR MINISTRY

1

Inherited concepts of leadership

A case study

HUGH CROSS

'A Bishop in all but name', ran the headline on the Press Release announcing my appointment in November 1990 to be the first Ecumenical Moderator of Milton Keynes. It was a risky line to take, as was demonstrated by the fact that no sooner had the release landed on my doormat than I had a phone call from one of the church leaders for Milton Keynes wishing to make it clear that the appointment carried no suggestion of authority and no possibility of jurisdiction.

In fact it demonstrated how this new appointment was breaking new ground in terms of church leadership; that it was an experiment to see if there were other ways of leading than the inherited concepts with which we all have to work.

The origins

In the early 1970s, when hopes were high of Anglican/ Methodist unity, and the Congregational Church in England and the Presbyterian Church of England were nearly at the point of becoming the United Reformed Church, and the Areas of Ecumenical Experiment were about to become Local Ecumenical Projects (LEPs), people working together in Swindon looked at the question of ecumenical church leadership. They had had the experience of an informal practice of such ecumenical leadership by Bishop Freddie Temple, Bishop of Malmesbury. Drawing on that experience, and applying theological principles to the question, they produced the significant report, 'A Bishop for All Churches in Thamesdown'. Sadly it was not implemented for a number of reasons, but it was not entirely lost, for it became one of the seminal documents in the emergence in Milton Keynes, nearly fifteen years later, of the first Ecumenical Moderator.

In 1967, when Milton Keynes was designated to be the new city to be built in north Buckinghamshire, the Bishop of Oxford, Harry Carpenter, had the foresight to gather his fellow church leaders and draw up a policy for a pattern of working in the new city which would be based on the Lund dictum of doing everything together that was possible, and doing separately only those things that could not be done together. As progress was made, the Milton Keynes Christian Council was formed and its structure included a presidency of five denominational church leaders serviced by an ecumenical officer, The Rev Gethin Abraham-Williams. In order to meet the difficulty of the ecumenical demands made by the new city on church leaders with much wider areas of responsibility, they established the role of the Pastoral President. The Pastoral President was one member of the Presidency who, for a period of two years, acted on behalf of all the Presidents as a focus of unity and in a representational way.

It was out of the experience of how well this worked that the idea was born to have a pastoral president who would live in the city, fulfil the leadership requirements, would enjoy equality of status with the Presidents, and effectively be the 'bishop of Milton Keynes'.

What about authority?

The documents indicate that there was considerable discussion about what title to give the post. As can be seen from the story with which this chapter began, the use of the term 'bishop' had its own risks. On the one hand those from episcopal traditions would have certain expectations arising from inherited experience and theological understandings of episcopacy as it has developed. On the other hand those from traditions which have historically not been episcopally

ordered might have negative expectations of episcopacy arising from experiences which led to the practice of personal
episcopacy being positively discarded.

The title 'Ecumenical Moderator' was decided on even
though it used a formal description of pastoral oversight
used by the Reformed confession. At least 'moderator'
carries with it no hint of power, authority, or jurisdiction.

Although the post was established by the churches at a
regional level, it was done with the collaboration of the
churches locally. None of the Presidents could hand over any
of his own authority or jurisdiction, so any authority the
Ecumenical Moderator had would have to be earned, and
certainly could not have any element of juridical content.
There was scope for personal leadership without it being
circumscribed by denominational expectations, since the
post was ecumenical, and required ecumenical balance to be
preserved. The post was clearly that of the pastoral president, and the exercise of the task was to be undertaken in the
collegiality of the Presidency of the Milton Keynes Christian
Council.

The Swindon report had described the Bishop for all
churches in Thamesdown as having authority 'exercised in
Council', and had described how this would be exercised in
the context of a 'missionary council'. In taking over the idea,
Milton Keynes had structured the role into its pattern of
working as a council. The Ecumenical Moderator would
preside at meetings of both the Presidency and of the
Assembly, in a structure which demonstrated that they are
two equal parts of the whole Council. There was provision
also for a Lay Chair of the council, who would share with the
Ecumenical Moderator in presiding at meetings of the
Executive and of the Assembly. The Lay Chair is elected for
a two year term. The practice of the first five years of the
experiment has been for the Lay Chair to preside at meetings
of both Executive and Assembly, the Ecumenical Moderator
acting as a kind of assessor/consultant. The principle underlying this practice is that of collaborative ministry, whereby
leadership is exercised by the Ecumenical Moderator-in-
Council, a sharing between ordained and lay in the leadership and decision making of the churches.

Thus it may be seen that the Ecumenical Moderator enables the church leaders to work together, coming as they do from a variety of traditions which have different expectations of leadership and episcope and episcopacy. The Ecumenical Moderator is also, on behalf of the Presidency (because he/she is also a president), providing a collaborative style of leadership within the council by sharing leadership with the Lay Chair, and with the elected Executive which comprises a mix of ordained and lay people.

A pastoral role

Just as authority has to be earned, so does the privilege of being pastor pastorem. The appointment of an ecumenical moderator does not cut the lines between ordained ministers and their own denominational leaders. 'Receive the cure of souls, which is both yours and mine' is still used by the bishop in inducting an Anglican priest to her or his parish in Milton Keynes, whether it is in an LEP or a purely Church of England parochial appointment. That link cannot be severed. What is possible, however, is for the Ecumenical Moderator, because he/she is not part of the line management or disciplinary structure of the Church of England, to be available to hear the confidences of individual clergy who feel able to share at a very deep level without fear of such confidences affecting their future careers. The same is true for clergy of all the other confessions.

The role of the pastor is not simply that of one who hears confessions, but also one who knows the clergy and makes it an important element in the role of Ecumenical Moderator to know the clergy and their families so that a proper care is taken of the carers.

No one person could be expected to know everybody in every one of the sixty six congregations which together form the Milton Keynes Christian Council. The Ecumenical Moderator has the responsibility, nevertheless, to be aware of the way local leadership is being exercised, the direction in which congregations are working (or are not working), the particular challenges which face each congregation or group of congregations. Simultaneously the Ecumenical

Moderator's pastoral function includes knowing what the denominational councils at local level, e.g. the Circuit, the Deanery, the URC District, are doing and what challenges they face. The Ecumenical Moderator has ex officio a right to attend any denominational meeting in the area as part of the oversight exercised on behalf of the denominations.

A further example of team or collaborative ministry being exercised by the post holder may be seen in the way the Ecumenical Moderator shares his/her ministry with the Denominational Relations Group. This is a small group appointed by the denominations to be advisors to the Ecumenical Moderator on denominational matters and to help interpret denominational decisions and directions.

A teacher

It was said of Jesus that people were 'astounded at his teaching, for he taught them as one having authority, and not as the scribes' (Mark 1.22). Vincent Taylor, in his commentary on Mark, suggests that the power Jesus was showing was that of the prophet, and the astonishment was because the voice of prophecy had long been silent in Israel.

In the context of a new city in which the churches have consciously determined to work together in a covenanted way, it becomes necessary to try to discover the word of God for the life of the city and of the churches. The Ecumenical Moderator will be the enabler who helps the churches to exercise their prophetic role as a community in the wider community of society at large. The bishop may be a prophet, and if he does make prophetic statements he does so because he is seen as a leader of his community, exercising the corporate prophetic role of the community. In this respect the Ecumenical Moderator's role is similar to that of the bishop.

As teacher the role of the Ecumenical Moderator does differ in another respect from that of the inherited concept of the bishop. The bishop's role is to guide his community by being the interpreter and guardian of his church's teaching, and to instruct those coming new to the faith on the doctrinal basis of the church. The Ecumenical Moderator has the specific responsibility to know the teaching of all the churches and be able to interpret one to the other, and on occasion to be the arbiter in things ecumenical when disagreement becomes dominant and threatening. It is at this point that the job description's statement that the Ecumenical Moderator will 'challenge the denominational structures to engage increasingly in joint decision-making in the pursuit of our common mission' applies.

A new kind of leadership

The first five years of the role of Ecumenical Moderator have demonstrated that such an office can be fulfilled within the churches, and have given signs of how it can be exercised.

The World Council of Churches' document on 'Baptism, Eucharist and Ministry' described ordained ministry as being exercised personally, collegially and communally. In line with that international ecumenical understanding of ordained ministry, the role of the Ecumenical Moderator can be identified, while at the same time providing an opportunity in practice to re-examine inherited concepts of leadership.

2

Pastoral theology re-defined

Correspondence between

GILLIAN STAMP *and* NORMAN TODD

Dear Gillian,
We were each asked separately for an article on the same subject: 'Research leading to training in order to redefine pastoral theology'. However, having often worked together it seems better to tackle the subject together in the form of a correspondence. This would be more likely to discover what correspondence there is between our two disciplines in this area. It might also demonstrate the dialogue which MODEM exists to promote. The new title I have suggested would be a more modestly realistic contribution to any redefinition of pastoral theology whether or not it is 'discovered' in the secular or religious disciplines.

A glance at the shelf labelled 'Pastoral Theology' in any religious bookshop would reveal a selection dealing with the casualties of life; how to counsel people in some form of psychological or emotional crisis. Indeed the shelf label would be 'Pastoral Care'. There is a library of Pastoral Care. There are diocesan advisers in the subject, mostly concerned with the practice of counselling people with personal problems. There is also a fairly recent history of attempts to redefine pastoral theology (e.g. Thornton, McIntosh, Hiltner, Ballard, Rahner).

I imagine that in management and business studies neither 'pastoral' nor 'theology' would appear. Casualties fall by the wayside or, it is hoped, into the common welfare net.

Theology would mean irrelevant as when a business man hoped that 'no more of these irrational theological objections would arise'. He was commenting on the decision not to sink the Brent Spar oil rig. 'Pastoral' would be taken to mean romantically rural. Any association with shepherds would depend on T.V. sheep dog trials in which, usually a man directs one or two dogs by whistles and shouts to scare a small group of ewes over an obstacle course. Not a correct image for a manager, nor for a minister, though it may be nearer the truth than either of them like to admit.

Shepherding has, of course, been a widely used metaphor for leadership in the churches. As John Adair points out (p. 61) it was not used much outside the Bible. The shepherd in Israel led his sheep, called them by name, maintained the unity of the flock, and met the individual needs of the sheep. Jesus is the Good Shepherd who knows his sheep (and other flocks) and will defend them with his life – unlike the hireling who runs away when there is danger. Adair also points out that 'good' means skilful rather than morally good.

I believe we should regain the full metaphor in the church. A variety of metaphors can be even more useful (Morgan). But we need to go beyond that and use the secular disciplines of a more scientific approach. I know from the work we have done together that your systems approach can apply to the organisation of the church. There are certain basic structures in varying proportion in all organisations arising from the nature of human relationships. In fact even 'corporate' and 'organization' are metaphors. Therefore I prefer to examine people in relationships (P-in-R) rather than sheep whether they are outside or inside the church. We are then more likely to see what is happening and use any influence to promote effectiveness and well-being.

Yours sincerely,

Norman

*   *   *

Dear Norman,

Your comment that 'theology seems to have dropped out' set me thinking about the increasing amount of shelf-space in general bookshops given to texts on 'personal growth' geared not so much to 'casualties' as towards people taking responsibility for understanding and developing themselves. You also say that neither 'pastoral' nor 'theology' would appear in books on management or business studies, but what does appear are words like 'care, nurture, foster, coach'.

There is a catch here or, as Americans would say, an 'up' and a 'downside'. The 'upside' is a recognition that the time has come for organisations to treat people as people – to 'empower' them. Global flows of capital and information and increasing competitiveness, make organisations very vulnerable unless they delegate decision-making to the levels where people have direct access to economically significant on-the-spot information (this is the essence of the quality movement).

Global, financial capitalism is a profound paradox: competitiveness demands that people should be treated as people; currency and information flows mean it does not matter which people or where they live. 'People are our most precious resource' and 'production will be transferred to dollar denominated currencies' may seem incompatible but both are the current reality. The economist's view is simple – there are losers and gainers; parts of Bangalore are now thriving because software design work is done well and cheaply there; unemployment in parts of Europe is 12%.

Living with the apparent paradox that people are important but individuals are interchangeable calls for some kind of support – pastoral? How is a manager to make sense of the expectation that she will both coach the people who work to her and reduce the headcount? That he will maintain long-term relationships with preferred suppliers and 'pin them on price'? What does it mean to manage people one never sees? Are they 'virtual employees' and, if so ...?

The downside' is that for those who remain in employment, contracts are being rewritten to the advantage of the employer, empowering is rarely accompanied by clarity about accountability and thus leads to mutual suspicion, there is a risk that people are treated not as people but as 'brains' – as one management 'guru' put it 'if we believe this stuff about the brain-based economy, then the brain is the only asset you've got'. At the same time there are huge redundancy programmes, with all the insecurity they induce.

Together these lead to inevitable cynicism and disillusion, often compounded by what is called 'culture change.' This is undertaken when an enterprise wants to make the most of the value of information and to minimise the costs of communicating it. In order to achieve this it has to treat people as people and so it introduces changes in the kinds of opportunities for, and control, over them. The idea is to make it less likely that they will act opportunistically and use the information for their own purposes, more likely that they will share it constructively and thus increase its value for the organisation as whole.

Again, there is an upside and a downside. The positive benefit is that organisations are drawn to think about issues like vision, values, trust, reciprocal relationships, quality, care for customers, shareholders, employee development, even the spirit of the enterprise. The difficulty is that these age-old issues about people-in-relationships starkly raise the delicacies and difficulties of treating people as people – and not as parts i.e. 'hands', 'brains', 'consumers'.

People treated as people (or as 'human human beings' as one shopfloor worker put it to me) soon want to make a contribution, to do things their own way. Their unquestioning loyalty is replaced by pointed questions; creativity sought after precisely because it will produce something new, becomes feared because it adds to unpredictability, everything seems to 'slip out of control', no matter how hard managers try to find out what 'makes them tick' each person remains a mystery.

In the face of these difficulties, it is neither surprising nor blameworthy that organisations retreat into rhetoric. They talk – and publish glossies — about co-operation, shared destiny, inclusivity, the importance of reciprocal relationship and long-term contracts, of delegated decision-making. In one way they really mean it, they know they have to do these things for competitive advantage. But much of the behaviour of investors [witness the pensions funds], of directors, of top managers [witness share options, huge salary increases, wide salary differentials] sends a clear message of individualism and greed, grab all you can, go when the going's good – and exploit.

This leaves people at all levels 'on the horns of dilemmas' – look after oneself or collaborate? work towards an individual performance bonus or for the good of the team? treat people like people or as 'units'? respond to the customer and be penalised for not answering 'enough' calls (for instance, BT pays bonuses according to the number of calls answered while, at the same time, preaching responsiveness to the customer).

It is in trying to find a way to live with all this that people need care and support which could be pastoral and possibly spiritual. But, returning to my point at the beginning about people taking responsibility for their own growth and looking for interdependence in relationships, I would like to suggest a slightly different gloss on 'pastoral' which could, as you put it, 'regain the full metaphor'. Perhaps being a pastor (pascere – to feed, to furnish with food, to allow to grow) is about leading people to spaces, places, times, ideas, methods where they can nourish themselves to live with paradox.

So we go beyond pastoral as dependent – sheep blindly following or being driven by a barking dog – to the act of guiding towards a place where the sheep can feed and sustain themselves ('Sheep may safely graze'). One can extend the metaphor in that they may need to be led to higher pastures, brought down in the winter, the wind tempered to the shorn lamb etc. But the essence is leading to a place where each is in a position to look after him or herself (there is a link here with the way in which each individual must now take responsibility for the path of their own working life and for developing the skills and gaining the experience he or she will need.) Perhaps the assumption needs to shift away from 'flock' back to the Latin 'grex' and from dependent to gregarious.

Your idea of People-in-Relationships makes great sense to me. I would want to have a subset of People-in-Working

Relationships (P-in-WR) because my experience suggests that there are particular qualities in the kinds of relationship that underlie working together and that these seem to be much the same whether people arc paid, receive a stipend or give their time, and in very different kinds of enterprises and diverse cultures.

In my experience people genuinely want to work within optimal conditions and to provide them for others, but pressures, inconsistencies, confusions and growing concern for their own positions 'lead them astray'. They are 'tempted' by a longing for certainty and control, for truth rather than mercy. And they are afraid of putting themselves 'out on a limb' by managing in a different way from those in the organisation who have the power to affect their future.

You are familiar with my Tripod of Work which describes a way of making provision for people to work as people, acknowledging the mutual dependency of interdependence. In essence, the Tripod is a pattern of P-in-WR grounded in the idea of 'do as you would be done by' – an inspiration that seems to be held in common by most religious and cultural traditions.

In the Tripod people task and are tasked – share intention, limits and resources; trust and are trusted with the purpose ('vision') of the organisation and to use their best judgement in serving it; tend and are tended – provide and use the space, the information, the waiting upon (ministering), the watching over (episcope) that keep the enterprise on course.

The outcome of tasking, trusting and tending should be (i) coherence of direction, energy and understanding; (ii) discernment of wise courses of action, (iii) review – an inbuilt capacity to pause, forgive and learn. Thinking about what people tell me of their lives at work now, this optimal tripod begins to look completely unrealistic, a dream rather than an aspiration. And yet there may be a journey towards it or something like that?

Will be thinking more about P-in-WR in the next couple of weeks. In the meantime where I think I've got to is:
(a) an attempt to think of 'pastoral' not as in herding a

flock, but as leading people to a place (and/or a time) where they can nourish themselves;

(b) an urgent need for 'pastoral' support for people living with the dilemmas of their present working lives: moral dilemmas about what they do, spiritual concerns about 'what it all means'.

With best wishes,

Gillian

*   *   *

Dear Gillian,

The dilemmas you describe as arising in so many secular organisations (yes, I agree with P-in-W-R though I am not sure if they are really so different, just more skewed) seem very similar to those dealt with in traditional pastoral theology. They occur when we have to walk two divergent ways at the same time, when we cannot abandon one or the other. The struggles of managers towards the ideal tripod of Tasking, Trusting and Tending sound like the biblical search for the 'promised land'. The escape from Egypt to the freedom and peace of the promised land was eventually realised to be a delusion – though a definite improvement on the slavery of the pyramids. The exodus became a symbol or type for the real escape from the inevitable frustrations of life as it is to life as we feel it should be; in a word, hope.

The history and symbolism of Israelites provided the background of Jesus thought and action; especially escape from bondage of the rule of the evil one to the rule or kingdom of the God with whom he was identified.

It was leadership for people making this escape (salvation) that pastoral theology was about. The Pastoral Epistles (to Timothy and Titus) are about how the new P-in-W-R was being organised, how to receive the influx of grace, the new help available, for ordering a godly community; the Kingdom in waiting, as it were. Although there is always the temptation to escape by withdrawing from the world I think it is clear that the New Testament teaches being in the world, but not of the world, not conforming to the ways of the world, being transformed in order to transform. It was, and always will be, a struggle, though the Christian experience is that final victory is assured.

The classical text is the Pastoral Rule of St Gregory the Great, influential since the seventh century and still used today (e.g. by Archbishop Michael Ramsay). It describes the awe-full responsibility of such guidance and the exacting demand on the spiritual life of the pastor. It is as if qualities of good leadership are raised to the nth degree for this matter of life and death for P-in-W-R. The advice is for people living normal everyday life. Finally: 'When you penetrate the sublimest things, remember you are a man [sic]; for when you are enraptured above yourself, you will be recalled in anxiety to yourself by the curb of your own infirmities.'

You are right to insist that the sheep must be encouraged to find their own food. Indeed I remember Bishop Ian Ramsay lecturing church leaders on the need to move from prescriptive to exploratory theology. This is happening to some degree in most churches though there is still the craving for certainty provided by external authority especially among fundamentalists of any religion. Spiritual direction is more about being helped to find your own direction than having it dictated. But we are still very fundamentalist about the organisation of our church, and suspicious of any green shoots appearing among us.

I was struck by the mention in his last book by W. Edwards Deming (the Anglo-American guru of Japanese business) of the need for fundamental change in management. It was from mutually destructive competition (Win-Lose) to mutually cooperative support (Win-Win) and the word he used was 'metanoia'. It is a transliteration of the Greek word for 'repent' in the New Testament: 'repent and believe the good news'. This repentance or turning, he says, 'is essential, has to be maintained and has to spread through the organisation'. Deming was well aware of the religious meaning of the word but he uses it in a completely secular connotation and extends it to the whole of life including education. In your terms he seems to accept the up-side of capitalism and neglect the downside. Without spiritual metanoia I doubt if the whole world can become Win-Win, and yet ...?

So who cares for the carers, pastors the pastors, rules the rulers if they are not to be the blind leading the blind? It is not enough to say 'God' or 'Christ' when the words do not contain the power for people. The sustenance has to be there within the struggle, incarnate in the metanoia and pilgrimage to the promised land of (in the case of both secular and religious organisations) the Optimal Tripod of Tasking, Trusting and Tending (TTT) for all P-in-W-R.

I wonder if another tripod can helps us here. F. von Hügel taught that there are three forces or elements of the human soul (i.e. the essential human being). Each has to be held in balance by the other two. The first is the Institutional by which we maintain continuity in community and society. The second is the Critical by which we analyse and attempt to synthesise our experience. The third is the Mystical. And this is the main theme of his writing I quote. The Mystical element is the faculty 'by which we have an however dim yet direct and [in its effect] immensely potent, sense and feeling, an immediate experience of Objective Reality, of the Infinite and Abiding, of a Spirit not unlike yet distinct from our own, which penetrates and works within these our finite spirits and in the world at large, especially in human history' (p. 387 f).

Perhaps it is the Mystical Element which is being excluded from our organisations so that the other elements become inflated. If so an essential part of P-in-W-R is represented only by its absence – something, we know not what, is missing. And is this the food that gives sustenance for the journey through the wilderness to the land of which the promise lies within every human being?

With all best wishes
Yours sincerely,

Norman

         *   *   *

Dear Norman,

It seems to be the questions we ask each other that help most. Your questions from outside my usual frame of reference force me to recognise almost the same kind of question from within it. The correspondence helps me to 'suspend my certainties', helps us to respect each other and thus really to work *together* rather than just adding our thinking and models. You encourage me to think more deeply to frame responses that might satisfy you and certainly help my way of thinking and the way I offer that to other people.

For instance, I would not have thought in terms of pastoral theology/care/rule and, without that stimulus, would not have begun to see the journey imagery of the tripod.

I see glimmers of further important coherences and look forward to your responses. For instance, I begin to have a sense that there is some sort of connection between tasking, trusting and tending and the institutional and critical elements of von Hugel's tripod. Your suggestion that the mystical element is an absence in many organisations makes me think about the relationship of the three Ts with the purposes, values and beliefs on which they rest. This needs more thought.

The analogy you draw between the three Ts and the promised land is interesting, especially for the insight that the 'escape' was a delusion and that the 'promised land' is about hope. As I've said, managers do seem to be hoping for hope through their struggles, and even facing questions of faith – although they would not usually put that in religious terms.

Your comments helped me to think of a 'journey' of P-in-WR aiming towards the optimal but deviating or being deflected along the way. Are deviations from the route to the promised land 'temptations' and/or spiritual confusions, or just the intrinsic vulnerability of human nature? The present starting point for that journey is the history of capitalist patterns of working relationships.

As the political scientist A. Hirschmann pointed out, capitalism has within it tendencies that both reinforce and undermine social fabric. For example, the constant practice of commercial transactions generates feelings of trust and empathy between people who see themselves as equal, 'all in the same boat'; but such practices permeate all spheres of life with the element of calculation and instrumental reason. This paradox is sharply visible in public services where the concept of the market has been imposed in order to provide improved service, yet many service purchasers and providers can feel they are morally compromised.

In the eighteenth century, the tendencies in capitalism that reinforced the social fabric were described as 'doux commerce', the phrase encapsulating a new morality to counteract exploitation by landowners. 'The great enforcer of morality in commerce is the continuing relationship'. In the late twentieth century the emphasis on the economically beneficial effects of relationships have been described by a professor at the London Business School as 'organisational architecture' – the network of relationships outside and inside the organisation that confer competitive advantage. Relationships are also the key to the 'inclusivity' advocated by the report on Tomorrow's Company recently published by the Royal Society of Arts.

Are there ways in which pastoral and theological under-standings could be used to help managers make the most of the reinforcing tendencies of capitalism? Not to rail against executive salaries and unemployment but to help institutions and people build on the potential for different kinds of rela-tionship less dependent, deferential and self-protecting than those that have emerged through industrial capitalism; patterned more along the webs of mutual self-interest that characterise commerce and therefore, perhaps, financial capitalism.

Reaching that point made me think more about the increasing need to treat people as people in order to make the most of information as it is recaptured from technology to become the prime currency of management: as one writer puts it 'information is the raw material for meaning and thus for management'. 'Processing information' could be done by 'brains' but will be far better achieved by people. Similarly, information can be disseminated through many different media, but sharing information – especially the tacit infor-mation that is the key to team work – is best done through relationships built and sustained by people. Information systems are invaluable in gathering information once they know where to look, excellent at storing it once they have been told what to capture. Increasingly they can spot trends and recurring patterns, but they lack human discernment.

And so treating people as people will be of the essence, the rhetoric will be forced to become the reality. And the ethic – in its Sanskrit derivation as 'placing' – will be the way the enterprise and the individual place themselves in the environment. All the complexities, the unpredictability and irreversibility of peoples' actions will have to be addressed. People are *makers* of meaning and of decisions *members* of many groups of which their employing organisation is only one and increasingly remain members of a particular enterprise for only as long as it suits them or the organisation. People are irreducibly *mysterious*. And, as someone said to me after I had spoke about these three 'Ms', 'Would you like another "M"? Treating people as people is *messy*!'

Perhaps both individuals and organisations would benefit from some pastoral preparation for the response to what is likely to be an economic imperative for P-in-WR rather than P-W (parts at work). Organisations will probably have to work with fewer people who are full or part time staff, more who are contractors, more from diverse cultures, but all will expect – and hope – to be treated as P-in-WR. Meeting that expectation will confer competitive advantage. The amount of resource being put into teamwork training in many organisations can be seen as part of this preparation and it is interesting how often that leads to questions about meaning, purpose, values – 'spirit' something akin to von Hugel's mystical element.

Let me end this letter by asking you some questions about P-in-WR in the church. Ministering to the potential and mysteries of people in relationship (P-in-R) seems to be one of the areas in which the church has such rich thought, teachings, experience and, in a way, so much suffering because the reality seems to slip so often, so far from the aspiration.

You once told me that Bishops at their consecration hear the words of Christ: 'Feed my lambkins. Shepherd my lambs. Feed my lambkins'. How do they feed them? How would they know they've done it? Could they measure it? – no, I'm not serious, just thinking of how helpful some of the performance management disciplines are in secular organisations. More seriously – is there something in the food Bishops can provide and/or in the way they provide it – in the right pasture for the season? that gives more or different sustenance? There is pitifully little available for managers as they struggle with their dilemmas, uncertainties, insecurities.

One very important attitude and behaviour that moves readily and with considerable added value from religion to secular enterprises is the notion of *forgiveness*. As Hannah Arendt pointed out, Jesus of Nazareth made it clear that forgiveness is the only way society can take account of the irreversibility of peoples' actions; without it each person would be locked into their deeds forever and there would be no innovation, no creativity, no learning. As you know 'the learning organisation' is currently an important aspect of thinking about organisations, but without forgiveness, blame rules and learning cannot take place.

What other notions can be carried across for mutual enhancement of management and ministry?

With best wishes,

Gillian

*   *   *

Dear Gillian,
You are right to ask what the food is and whether the results of its nourishment are apparent in the church. There is a danger that rhetoric is used as a substitute for food instead of a possible aid to digestion. And I do not think we should refuse all attempts to measure the results as long as we remember the dangers of measurement seen in the management of health and education where there can be a switch to

producing the test requirements instead of what they are measuring. Spiritual health may be more difficult to assess than physical but can, with due humility be attempted. I believe that there has been a real improvement in the quality of spiritual guidance in the churches I know, and of saintliness despite much publicised failures. The adverse criticism, even when unbalanced, may do some good. Judgement really does 'begin at the household of God', because that is where any failure is most glaring.

But without in any way losing the gains which have been made in bringing spiritual and practical resources to individual people in need and to individual sanctity, we must give equal attention to corporate health and sanctity within the P-in-W-R which is the church. Here the pastoral metaphor may now be a hindrance. The congregation within the parish is not much like a flock. Rather it consists of concentric rings of people in varying degrees of maturity and commitment. It has all the complexity, all the deep structures of any set of P-in-W-R. This is why I am sure we can learn from you how to understand the way we work as a whole. Your TTT tripod is completely relevant especially as the church moves towards a much greater participation of all members in its own management.

The Mystical Element is not lacking but is not properly developed within the People of God as P-in-W-R. Indeed the church might see TTT as one reflection of the way we feel God is dealing with us, and an invitation to be blown with the Spirit. It was Michael Ramsay who argued that the church should by its shape express the Gospel. But so should every manifestation of P-in-W-R.

There are already benefits within the churches from the Management and Organisation Disciplines. Quality (ISO 9000) is described in a separate chapter in this book. However we need to collect together these 'Enhancements of Ministry' so that they can be tested, developed, applied more widely and the benefits included in training of clergy and congregations.

Will there be any Enhancement of Management by the Disciplines of Ministry? If there is, it will be from open dialogue such as these letters may demonstrate, not because the church thinks it has something to teach. Mutual discovery is the only way forward – which is what you mean by 'coherence' in your tripod and part of what we, in these letters mean by 'correspondence'.

The church grows by baptising new members, by facilitating their motivation throughout their lives; also by improving the quality of its common life. It grows also by influencing the world whose hopes and fears it shares, though from within its own experience. It can be, grow, influence, only by its practice; the way it works. Pastoral theology must be about this and how it can be made to work more effectively within the real world of dilemmas, paradox and chaos which appears at first to be entirely negative, but which eventually may be recognised as potential beauty. In theological terms this is about the transformation of nature by grace. This is not abstract but intensely practical.

There is another tripod, one of transformation, from St John of the Cross. Natural memory becomes hope. Natural understanding becomes faith. And natural will becomes love. From the human end the means of transformation is humility, the ability to experience others and oneself as they really are. We are again moving towards mysticism but the roots are there in the struggles of your managers just as much as in the struggles of the church.

There is room only for one last thought. There seems to be a sparsity of mature ministry and I wonder if there is any correspondence in management. A very able parish priest once told me of having been in a parish for about seven years and feeling he had done all he could. The bishop agreed it was time for a move. It was only after he had been in his next parish for some time that he was able to say, 'I wish the bishop had come and sat down with me and discussed what was happening after seven years. Then he or his ministry consultant would have worked with me building on my experience so far and planning the next phase of my own ministry and of the growth of the church there. Instead I went off and started from scratch somewhere else and someone came to start from scratch where I had been.' Perhaps this is an oversimplification but I think we need more experience of second – and third-phase ministry by clergy in the church and by the church in the parish (i.e. the catchment area whether territorial or sector).

With all best wishes and looking forward to your reply,

Yours sincerely,

Norman

*   *   *

Dear Norman,
You are right, it is both the questions I ask and my attempts to respond to yours that take us forward. Have been looking over our correspondence so far and can see running through – usually just below the surface – my theme of confusion between the moral and the spiritual. The dilemmas people in work talk about are of what to do in situations where there are double messages – be a coach and dismiss eighty people, delegate decision-making and trust no-one; build long-term relationships and exploit.

My sense is that people feel an underlying confusion, sometimes a distress that they are somehow being compromised, undermined by what they are asked to do at work. I am not thinking here of the more extreme situations of 'whistle-blowing' but of the daily small compromises that people experience as corrosive. If they have a live or even a latent belief – based in any religious tradition – in another way of doing things or another life after this one, that seems to provide at least fragments of a deeper reality. But when they espouse the 'dominant religion of the West – pragmatic materialism predicated on the assumption that this life is all there is', there *seems* to be an emptiness for them that they might like to fill but have no idea how to go about it. Is this 'awareness of an absence' the spiritual issue, is it the missing mystical element?

Something may emerge if I tell you about my further thinking about the journeying of P-in-WR and the tripods. The map is heralded 'Towards the Promised Land' and is liberally sprinkled with 'there be dragons'. The journey will require very considerable pastoral sensitivity and care for individuals, teams, sections, departments, divisions, organisations.

As you commented, most people seem to recognise the optimal tripod as 'the ways things should be' or almost as a version of 'do as you would be done by', but more and more I am finding that people respond to it as a dream, idealistic, very far from the reality of their daily working lives. That does not seem to stop them seeing it as an aspiration, something they would try to work towards – interestingly, often from a straight economic and business point of view with proper care for people and people in relationships taken as essential. For the moment they feel powerless to achieve it but they recognise it with a jolt almost of hope.

As an aside, why a tripod? a three-legged stool? I have recently been reading a book about the sacred nature of number where the author – the physicist David Peat – uses the example of a stool whose legs serve as an example of the movement towards harmony. It is not difficult for an amateur carpenter to make a serviceable three-legged stool, for as soon as you set it on the floor, it will be in balance. Even when its three legs are not exactly the same length, the stool will not rock and, even when the floor is uneven, it will be balanced. For a mathematician, the three points of the tips of the legs define a unique plane and it is a fundamental fact that it is always possible to put down a three-legged stool so that the tip of each leg just touches the floor. No other plane will touch the three tips of the legs; there is only one single orientation of balance, no other is possible. Is it going too far to connect the movement towards harmony with the hope in the image of a promised land?

To return to the journeys; there seems to be one from a tripod for P-in-WR in stable conditions (where there is not much uncertainty to cope with) towards the optimal tripod needed to make the most of change: towards your 'promised land'. For me it may or may not be 'in accord with the Will of God' but it certainly does seem to be a pattern of P-in-WR that induces mutual confidence, minimises suspicion and mutual recrimination and appears to be necessary to cope with rapid and unpredictable change.

In stable conditions it has traditionally been appropriate for managers to give instructions to their subordinates, deploy them for their skills and experience, expect them to make deductions, and, very occasionally, to use their judgement: to treat them as dependent and expect their loyalty; to make sure that administration is efficient and proper records are kept.

P-in-WR in stable conditions can be drawn in a Tripod of Continuity.

The Tripod of Continuity

An enterprise has to be placed in a very different way if it is to keep going in unpredictable, uncertain conditions; deduction cannot cope with irreducible uncertainty, loyal dependency limits the capacity to respond flexibly to change, record-keeping does not readily lend itself to learning. Making the most of unpredictable change requires discernment – 'patience with uncertainty' as you once told me it was described by a Bishop – to pick up on the regular irregularities that often thread through even the most chaotic conditions; coherence for immediate understanding of where energy can best be placed without having to wait for permission; review to provide an in-built capacity to learn from even the tiniest signals.

So, instructing must become tasking – shared intention, agreeing limits and resources. Deploying people must become entrusting with the 'vision' of the organisation and trusting them to use discernment in serving it. Administering must become tending – providing and using the space, the information that P-in-WR need to do their work, waiting upon them (ministering), watching over them (episcope) and keeping the enterprise on course.

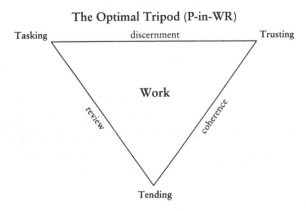

The Optimal Tripod (P-in-WR)

What seems to happen is that the first, inevitably uncertain wandering and often piecemeal steps towards the optimal tripod release energies and anxieties that threaten to overwhelm the capacity of the enterprise to absorb change.

As I said in an earlier letter, disillusion seems often to be the outcome of empowerment and culture changes that have, more often than not, started out with constructive change and customer-oriented assumptions. Faced with all the energy, irreversibility and unpredictability that is released when people are treated as people, the organisation retreats into rhetoric, sometimes imposes changes in behaviour on employees. The pattern of P-in-WR becomes one of cynicism and disillusion.

Even in these negative conditions, people often respond to the optimal tripod as in some way 'right' or 'fair' and do not lose hope although they may have no faith that the pattern of working relationships will ever really change in a deep way. It reminds me of the Larkin line which runs something like 'in each of us there lives a dream of a life lived according to love'.

My mind is now full of ideas, but there is no room in this letter. Ideas about the journeys that have to be made if P-in-WR are to move from 'deduction' to 'discernment' without

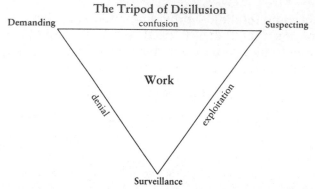

The Tripod of Disillusion

becoming lost in confusion, from 'loyal dependency' to 'coherence' and avoid exploitation, from 'record-keeping' to 'review' without becoming caught in denial. I am already making notes for our next correspondence.

Best wishes,

Gillian

*   *   *

Conclusion

(From Gillian Stamp and Norman Todd to the reader)

To some extent our letters have been devised and edited for publication. They are, however, based upon and typical of our regular correspondence. We realise we have failed to deal with the many issues we have raised and have left many questions unanswered. That is typical not only of correspondence but also of working life. We shall follow up some of them and invite you to do so as well.

As far as research is concerned, we suggest the following:

(A) *Ministry*
   1. Further deconstruction of the metaphors used to describe ministry.
   2. How does the church actually work? Construct models of what is actually going on.

3. How does the church, in its working experience and structure respond to and hence, in some measure express the presence of the tasking, trusting and tending of God?

(B) *Management*
4. How can the deeper human needs of P-in-R and P-in-WR be addressed?
5. How can we appraise the spirit of an organisation?
6. How can managers be supported as they sacrifice themselves for the common good?

(C) *Both*
7. Clarify the advantages of enhancement in both directions.
8. Develop this correspondence.

(D) Use secondments in both directions.

(E) Alert University Departments to these research opportunities

(F) Establish a data base and clearing house for work in the MODEM arena

We sign off with two quotations:

The differences between churches and factories
Everyone understands
It's the difference between the laying on and the laying off
Of hands
Gavin Ewart

God's Grace given freely, we do not deserve
But we can choose at least to see its ghost
On every face Oh, we can wish to serve
Each other gently as we live, though lost.
We cannot save, be saved, but we can stand
Before each presence with gentle heart and hand;
May Sarton

REFERENCES

Adair, J., *Great Leaders* (Talbot Adair, 1989).

Arendt, H., *The Human Condition* (The University of Chicago Press, 1958).

Ballard, P. H., *The Foundations of Pastoral Studies and Practical Theology* (Report of Working Party).

Deming, W. Edwards, *The New Economics* (MIT, 1993).

Hiltner, S., *Preface to Pastoral Theology* (Abingdon Press, 1958).

Hirschman, A.O., *Rival Interpretations of Market Society: Civilizing, Destructive or Feeble?* (Journal of Economic Literature, Vol. XX pp. 1463–1484).

McIntosh, I., *Pastoral Care and Pastoral Theology* (Westminster, 1982).

Morgan, G., *Images of Organisations* (Beverley Hills CA: Sage, 1986).

Peat, F.D. *Blackfoot Physics* (Fourth Estate Limited, 1995).

Rahner, K., *Theological Reflections Vol 19* (DLT, 1983).

Sarton, M., *A Hard Death* in R. Ainsley (ed) Death of a Mother: Daughters' Stories. (Pandora, an imprint of HarperCollins, 1994).

St Gregory the Great, *Pastoral Care*, trans H. Davis (Longmans Green 1950).

St John of the Cross, *Complete Work*, trans E. A. Pears of Vol 1 p. 445. (Burns Oates, 1935).

von Hügel, F., *The Mystical Element of Religion* of Vol 2 p. 387 F. (Dent, 1908).

3

Affirming lay ministries

RICHARD HIGGINSON

Much 'lay ministry' has been understood in terms of lay people taking a more active role in the life of the church. We now have more lay men and women preaching, leading services, taking intercessions, running home groups and doing baptism visits than generally used to be the case. Since, as St Paul wrote, the church is a body in which each member performs a crucial function (1 Corinthians 12), this is a development greatly to be welcomed. Often there are specific tasks in the church's life which seem precisely matched to a particular person's gifts. Perhaps the membership includes an advertising executive who makes a superb editor of the church magazine, or a currently out-of-work community worker who is marvellous at running the youth group. The message of the New Testament is clear: 'As each has received a gift, employ it for one another, as good stewards of God's varied grace' (1 Peter 4.10).

In all this, however, there are a number of prevalent dangers to be avoided.

One is to assume that individuals who practice a particular occupation day by day necessarily want to perform its church equivalent outside their working hours. It may be important that an accountant does *not* look after the church's finances, and a hard-pressed teacher does *not* teach in the Sunday school, in order that they keep themselves fresh for their weekday work. It would actually be better if someone else had a go at being treasurer or teaching the children, and that the accountant and teacher use or develop another gift in the context of their involvement in the church.

The second is to ignore the considerable pressures experienced by many people in their working lives, especially those
in management positions. Often their work (travel time
included) consumes twelve or more hours of the day; they
come home with their heads buzzing and feeling thoroughly
washed out. Those who stay at home (still usually the wife)
also reach the evening hours tired, but for different reasons,
typically the demands of small children. Couples in those
circumstances need to communicate, but this is not easily
done: time is required to unwind. The last thing they probably need is the demand of having to lead a house-group the
moment the husband walks in. It is all too easy for church
activities to add to the stress felt by Christian people. Church
leaders need to be sensitive to the existence of such pressures,
and to know when – gifted as a particular individual or
couple might be – asking then to fulfil a particular function
might drain their energies or strain their relationship to
breaking point.

The third danger is a failure to recognise that the things
people are doing Monday to Friday, nine till five (and often
longer) constitute genuine ministry in their own right. They
are an essential part of Christian discipleship. The ministry
of laypeople is something that happens in the world, and not
just in church. Sadly, the development of lay ministry in the
last twenty-five years has tended to obscure rather than high-
light that fact.

Too many Christians (surprisingly, even some in quite
senior positions) tend to regard work as a necessary evil, a
means of making ends meet so that one is then able to pursue
and finance the really interesting things which go on outside
working hours. Much of their time may be spent at work,
but most of their creative energy goes elsewhere, often into
activities of the church. Where that is the case, relating faith
to the work-place, and seeing it as an opportunity for
ministry, does not feature seriously on the agenda. It could be
a serious diversion from what it is thought Christians should
really be about: evangelising their neighbour and keeping
themselves 'unspotted' from the world, a duty which often
gets restricted in work-place terms into not swearing and not
stealing the paper-clips!

Positive understanding

In contrast, I would like to suggest a much more positive understanding of the relationship between faith and work. Daily work is a sphere for which God gifts people and to which God calls people. The talents with which God has equipped men and women include a fine eye for financial detail, skill in resolving conflict, and dexterity with one's hands. Talents like these can go a long way to making the world, not just the church, a significantly better place. Using the language of Martin Luther, the 'stations' in which we find ourselves (e.g., engineer, secretary, and social worker, as well as parent, spouse and councillor) can all constitute genuine vocations in which we are called to serve God and love our neighbour.[1]

Likewide, a positive understanding sees the summons of Jesus to be 'salt of the earth' and 'light of the world' as taking expression, first and foremost, in the place where people spend most of their time. So salt preserves and light warns: we have a responsibility to resist evil influences and alert to moral danger in the work-place. Salt flavours and light guides: we have a responsibility to enhance what is good and witness to Christ. Above all, salt glistens and light shines: we have a responsibility to be true to our nature, authentically, visibly Christian. Jesus doesn't actually give us the option of choosing when and where to be salt and light. If, sadly, salt becomes contaminated, so that it loses its saltiness, or light is perversely hidden, the verdict Jesus gives is unmistakable: good for nothing! (Matthew 5.13–16).

A similarly positive approach is implicit in Paul's words in Romans 12.1–2. Paul exhorts his readers to 'present your bodies as a living sacrifice, holy and acceptable to God, which is your spiritual worship'. The vision is holistic: everything Christians do should be fit for offering to God in his service. Paul continues: 'Do not be conformed to this world but be transformed by the renewal of your mind ...' Notice the radical language of *transformation*. Christians in the work-place should not unthinkingly go along with the world's way of doing things. As people whose minds have been and are being renewed, they are concerned to 'prove what is the will of God, what is good and acceptable and perfect'. 'Prove' in this context has the meaning of 'discern' i.e., identify through a process of weighing and testing. A renewed mind chews over issues carefully and prayerfully. It neither eschews fashionable opinion automatically nor follows it slavishly. It is no longer 'conformed', because fresh influences and fresh perspectives have been brought to bear upon the issues under consideration. The New Testament presents the Holy Spirit as the great source of personal renewal.

My experience is that it is those who work in business who are particularly in need of help and encouragement in seeing their work as a potential sphere for ministry. The church signals its indifference, hostility to or suspicion of business in all sorts of ways, not least its failure to pray for this aspect of life. In exploring the link between work and worship, I have carried out the following exercise with numerous groups. I have asked them how often they recall people in the following occupations being prayed for in church services? The answers given are remarkably consistent. They are, on average, as follows:

> Quite often: Nurse, Teacher, Politician
> Occasionally: Ambulanceman, Farmer, Policeman, Soldier, Union Leader
> Never: Bank Manager, Broadcaster, Company Chairman, Design Engineer, Salesperson, Solicitor.

A clear message comes through. The people whom the church prays for most regularly in its public intercessions are those who work in the 'caring services', in education, or in positions of political leadership. Every now and again it prays for those who are at the forefront of crisis situations (strikes, wars, droughts, etc.) or have the task of maintaining law and order. It hardly prays at all for those involved in any type of commercial activity. I believe this represents a serious imbalance. Laypeople and clergy together are often implicated in an unconscious conspiracy to keep this slice of national (or rather international) life off the agenda.

Legitimacy of business

What is needed to remedy this situation is not just a mental note to pray for business people more often, however. It is acceptance and 'ownership' of a full-orbed theology which recognises the place for business in God's purposes, which supports the basic legitimacy of business but also subjects it to searching questions. Through the project which I direct at Ridley Hall, the Ridley Hall Foundation, and a book which I wrote out of experience of that project, *Called to Account*[2], I have played a modest part in trying to fill that gap. The book presents a systematic overview of the world of business from a Christian perspective. Each chapter illuminates detailed business scenarios by the light of a different Christian doctrine (e.g., creation, fall, redemption, future hope). My conviction is that from the first statement of the creed to the last, Christian faith is relevant, excitingly, if sometimes unexpectedly relevant, to the pursuits we follow during the week. We need more preachers and teachers in the church who are convinced of that!

One image which Jesus used of the kingdom of heaven was that of *hidden treasure*. 'The kingdom of heaven is like treasure hidden in a field, which a man found and covered up; then in his joy he goes and sells all that he has and buys that field' (Matthew 13.44). A vibrant, relevant theology of work has something of the character of hidden treasure. It may not have an overt impact on most of the work people do most of the time. But it is well worth unearthing periodically in order to reassess one's goals, values and methods in the arena of work. It provides distinctive insights which will sometimes lead Christians down roads unpursued by other people. It sets work within the overall purposes of God, and no Christian should be absorbed with the here-and-now that he or she loses that wider perspective.

The Christian faith is actually a crucial piece of working data. It provides essential clues for understanding who people are, why things go wrong, and how situations can be changed for the better. If that seems a bold claim, it chimes in with an observation which I hear increasingly often, that the best in modern management theory is really Christianity in secular guise. There is a lot of truth in this. I recall a MODEM meeting where a Professor of Business Studies told a group of clergy that the organisational world is 'stealing your clothes'. I am often struck by the number of resonances between the best of secular thinking and Christian thinking. Sometimes the correspondence may be due to the fact that business gurus are Christians, though not writing explicitly as such. But often it is simply the fact that Christian concepts like forgiveness, servant leadership and peace of mind are key constituents in functioning effectively, and those who are shrewdest in their study of human organisations are honest enough to admit it.

However, Christian faith does not only provide a way of understanding. It provides a personal resource – that of Jesus Christ. The hidden treasure Christians have at their disposal is not just Christian theology; it is Christ himself. There are moments in reading modern business literature when one agrees entirely with the diagnosis but wants to cry out that there is an answer, a resource who is being sadly neglected. An example is Roger Evans' and Peter Russell's book *The Creative Manager*, where they comment that in view of the pressures managers are under, one of the most pressing needs of our time 'is to develop the capacity to be more at peace with ourselves; to find a still centre of inner stability and calm from which we can think and act with greater clarity and creativity'.[3] While Christians do not have any monopoly on inner peace, many can testify that a personal relationship with Christ fills precisely the niche that Evans and Russell speak about. Lay ministry in the secular world will often be content to communicate by deeds alone, but there are times when it is appropriate to speak directly of Christ, and this carries greater weight when his relevance is shown to matters that the world is bothered about.

NOTES

1. Luther's teaching in this area is helpfully summarised both in Paul Althaus, *The Ethics of Martin Luther* (Fortress, 1972) and Gustaf Wingren, *The Christian's Calling: Luther on Vocation* (Oliver & Boyd, 1958).

2. Richard Higginson, *Called to Account: Adding Value in God's World* (Eagle & Highland, 1993).
3. Roger Evans and Peter Russell, *The Creative Manager* (Unwin Paperbacks, 1990), p. 13.

4

Reclaiming vocation for the whole people of God

DAVID CLARK

The 1950s and 1960s rediscovered the laity. Suddenly, through the vigorous advocacy of a then energetic World Council of Churches, the laity, the people of God, were news. So too on the British scene 'God's frozen people', as Mark Gibbs and Ralph Morton once called them, became 'God's lively people'. Laity centres mushroomed, lay training boards appeared and a 'new reformation' was surely at hand.

Forty years on we know that those weighty 'isms' of the institutional church – 'parochialism', 'denominationalism' and above all 'clericalism' have again defied all attempts to redeem them. Despite the effort and energy put into industrial mission, the emergence of the basic Christian community movement, an impressive National Pastoral Congress of the Roman Catholic Church in Liverpool in 1980, and potentially far-reaching reports on the central role of the laity emanating from three major denominations in the late 1980s, we now seem back to square one. Indeed, so incestuous and moribund is our present approach to the ministry of the laity that one could argue that we are no longer even at square one.

In 1993 The Christians in Public Life Programme (CIPL) undertook and published *A Survey of Christians at Work*. Some 400 lay people in paid work from all denominations answered a comprehensive questionnaire. 92% of respondents saw their work as 'very much' or 'to some extent' a Christian vocation, 84% regarded their work as 'very much' or 'to some extent' a part of the mission of the church. Yet for only one denomination (Quakers) was their affirmation through worship, supportive pastoral care and relevant educational programmes rated overall by these lay respondents as even 'to some extent' adequate. So where do we go from here?

Vocation

We must begin, I believe, by reclaiming the word 'vocation' for the whole ministry of the whole people of God. 'Vocation', as a once potent religious concept, has been hijacked in two very destructive ways. On the one hand, it has been 'commercialised' by being limited to only those forms of work which can lead to paid employment. Thus a host of marketable 'national vocational qualifications' are being designed which relegate 'non-vocational' interests and skills to the back burner. On the other hand, an élitist dimension of 'vocation' still lingers on when it is applied to the so called professions – teaching, medicine, law and the church (meaning only the clergy of course) – set aside as special and respected forms of public service located within the particular institutions concerned.

These interpretations of vocation are both debilitating and divisive. They limit the term to a restrictive range of competences or to an exclusive group of people. Vocation in this sense is about achievement not commitment, about the status of the few not the potential of the many. In brief, vocation becomes a restrictive practice, not an inclusive calling.

For the liberation of the church to occur, we need to reclaim the word 'vocation' for the whole people of God. This is not to exclude the ordained or the religious orders, but to argue that the vocation of the laity is crucial to the mission and ministry of the church. Their calling is not secondary or subsidiary to that of the clergy, it is just as important and equally valid. Indeed, if we do not reinstate lay vocation to its proper place in the life of the church, continuing institutional decline and demise are inevitable.

Partnership

Lay vocation is first and foremost a call to partnership; the biblical word is covenant. CIPL's recent 'statement of conviction' puts it this way:

> We are called to be partners with God in his continuing work of creation with the personal, corporate and global spheres of life.
> We are called to be partners with Christ as he frees and empowers individuals, institutions and nations to fulfil their God-given possibilities.
> We are called to be partners with the Spirit as she works for justice, peace and the unity of mankind.
> We are called to be partners with all those who work to further human dignity within the bounds of our common humanity.

Such a calling is not so much to doing as to being. God first calls you and me, through an I-Thou relationship with him, and through the 'exchange of life' which goes with that, to realise the gift of our human possibilities. Lay vocation means that we are engaged, with God, in the task of becoming the person he intended us to be. Or as Hans Kung puts it very succinctly: 'Why should one be a Christian? In order to be truly human.'

Personhood

The vocation of the people of God is a call to personhood. As such it cannot be fulfilled in either individual or sectarian isolation. It is a vocation which, in its turn, must involve an invitation to others to discover their own truly human possibilities. This will take a wide diversity of tangible forms – offering a listening ear, giving sacrificially to good causes, working to provide human styles of management, seeking to create and sustain human cities, caring for the preservation of the planet working for justice and peace locally and globally. Through these means of grace a called laity will be calling all people to deeper understanding of what it is to be human, and to a commitment to make personhood a reality for all.

But this is only one side of the coin. For God's calling of you and me to personhood is constantly conveyed to us *by* others, Christians and non-Christians alike. Lay vocation is not about our discovering some elixir of life which we can then offer to others in a spirit of lady bountiful. It is about a shared journey in which we have to respond to God's call to personhood through our fellows, often (as in the stories of Jesus) unexpected and unattractive fellows, as fully as God is calling them to respond to us. Lay vocation, the call to personhood, is thus an 'all-in' affair. We are called by and respond to God's presence in and through others, even our enemies, just as often as we call them and await their response.

The Kingdom is not divided. It is the same Kingdom beyond the walls of the church as within it. We should not, therefore, be disturbed that God's call to personhood can come to us through the 'secular' as often as the 'sacred'; that we can learn as much, if not more, about the meaning of being human from those of other faiths and none as we can from our fellow Christians.

This does not mean that personhood is on offer everywhere we turn. Because we are part of a fallen humanity, we shall constantly come up against dehumanising forces and destructive principalities and powers. Here the Christian community has the immense privilege of the role model of Christ himself, fully divine yet fully human, to which to relate. But even so, as our risen Lord, he will be as present in the lonely crowd and among the poor and the marginalised as he is within the scriptures and the church itself.

Lay vocation, then, is about a shared call and mutual response to personhood, individually and communally. It is not primarily about communicating 'the faith', looking for conversions or building up the church, though all these things may be involved. Our vocation is to become a human race fully alive, and as Irenaeus once put it, thereby glorify God our creator.

The Call of the Ordained Ministry

So where does the ordained ministry fit into the frame? Those of us in this category have exactly the same vocation – for we too are human beings made in God's image. Our call, like that of every Christian, is the call to personhood –

maturity in Christ. We are not exempt from the journey – nor can we ignore God's call, through many not of the community of faith, to open our eyes to new horizons and new vistas.

If the call of the ordained is unique, it is only in that we have a special role in fostering and developing the personhood of the people of God, whose would-be holiness is simply another word for wholeness. Thus it is a dreadfully serious state of affairs if worship and pastoral care and Christian education (as CIPL's *Survey* indicated) do not enable the laity to be enriched and grow as persons. For where this development is not occurring, no Kingdom can come on earth as in heaven. So the rediscovery of the centrality of the vocation of the whole people of God for the sake of world as well as church is of paramount concern for every one of us.

5

Relationships in mixed gender parishes

ELIZABETH WELCH *and* DAVID GOLDIE

INTRODUCTION

I have worked in a mixed gender parish for over twelve years. And yet when I was approached to write on this topic, I realised that it was not the issue of gender that was to the fore in my thinking about the way relationships are shaped and developed in this particular parish. I work in a Local Ecumenical Partnership, and it has been issues to do with ecumenism and with personality that have defined the boundaries and cutting edges of team life.

But first, to go back a step. I am a United Reformed minister, ordained in 1976. I come from a tradition that has been ordaining women to the ministry since the First World War. This has given me a particular perspective on the role of women in ministry, and the possibility of women and men working together.

Since 1983 I have worked at the Church of Christ the Cornerstone, Milton Keynes. This is a 5-denominational Local Ecumenical Partnership, involving Baptists, the Church of England, Methodists, the Roman Catholic Church, and the United Reformed Church. While Roman Catholic Masses are held separately, Anglican and Free Church people worship jointly. There are also shared non-Eucharistic services involving people of all the traditions. A varied pattern of weekday work takes place, as the church seeks to fulfil its role as the City Church for Milton Keynes.

This includes such things as running a coffee shop and book-shop, supplying 'duty ministers' each weekday to care for people dropping in to the building, and developing both a ministry to the growing congregations that come to the church, and to the city centre shops and offices amongst whom the church is set.

The life of the team has varied over the years since I arrived. When I first came, there were already 2 Anglican priests (male) in post (STAGE A). After three years one of these left, and we were then joined by a Roman catholic sister. She was part of the team for six years (STAGE B). During her last year we were joined by another Anglican priest (male) (STAGE C). The team now comprises 2 Anglican priests (male), a Methodist minister (male), another Roman Catholic sister, and myself (STAGE D).

In this chapter, one of the Anglican priests, Canon David Goldie, who has been here since the beginning of the project, and I, want to share some reflections on the kind of team ministry experience that we have had over these past twelve years. In discussion, we came to realise that the issues that have been primarily before us over these years, providing the cutting edges to the way in which the team has related, have more to do with denomination and personality than gender.

We will share a short reflection from each of us in relation to the particular question of gender, and then go on to develop issues to do with Denomination, and with Personality.

GENDER (*As seen by Elizabeth*)

I enjoy working in a mixed gender team. There are times when there is a certain buzz in the way we can relate as men and women together which livens up our discussions. There are times when we are able to share a breadth of different perspectives which deepens our thinking and understanding.

My experience has been that a mixed gender team has been found helpful by members of the congregation. It has given people a range of possible team members to relate to, and has, on occasion, meant that women have felt a confidence in talking to another woman, as have men in talking to another man. There have also been times when women from other congregations with an all male leadership, have deliberately come to Christ the Cornerstone in order to experience the leadership of a woman in ministry.

The particular gender issue on which the team has not always been of a common mind, and where we have divided down male/female lines, has been the issue of inclusive language. Somehow, it has seemed more easy for women to perceive the need for inclusive language than for men, even men who have a strong orientation towards being positive about women in ministry.

GENDER (*As seen by David*)

It hardly seems that gender has been a strong element in our team dynamic. There might have been the occasional moments in Stage A when the two Anglican men related to the URC woman in a way which corresponded to gender stereotypes. There might have been times in Stage B when each of the women was seeking the agreement of the man (and vice-versa) in a way which some analysts might consider to have inter-gender undertones; for example, was there any basic 'pairing' aspect to the way in which the women seemed to compete to have the man 'on board' their point of view? However, the strong impression is of team personalities which conform so little to the common stereotypes that gender dynamics seem largely absent.

There is the interesting question why the team personalities do conform so little to the common stereotypes. Is there perhaps a way in which the Christian call is heard as a call to develop their gentle side by some men and their leadership strengths by some women – or are we each letting the favourite details of the call reinforce our preferred modes of behaviour?

DENOMINATIONAL TRADITION

In every ecumenical partnership there is the discerning of the 'heart of the matter' things about which there is agreement and those areas where there needs at least at first to be the agreement to disagree. Our experience has been of

considerable convergence over matters of initial difference so
that we can come to appreciate the point and practice of
other traditions – the centrality of the eucharist, the baptism
of infants and of believers, the importance of preaching, the
value of hymnody, the reservation of the sacrament, different
forms of church government. Of course convergence takes
time: it was only after some years that Anglicans realised that
Methodists were offended to be collecting people's offerings
during a hymn, the balance between what decision-making
should happen in the congregational meeting and what in the
church council had to be adjusted as we grew from 30
through 130 to 230, and it took us well over a year's painful
discussion before there was a clear consensus that being
ecumenical involved having the reserved sacrament.

Perhaps it was particularly in Stage B that we tried to cope
with a number of issues which were new to us. Having a
Roman Catholic sister in the team who had given her life to
many aspects of Catholic devotion forced us not only to be
very aware of what these devotions meant to her but to
understand how important they were to many Catholics.
Any suggestion that something should be moderated out of
ecumenical sensitivity was felt to be a trampling on her soul,
but the good effect of this was to encourage all of us to check
that we had not watered down any of our own traditions
which were in fact important to us and enriching of one
another. It has to be said than when a second Roman
Catholic sister replaced the first one the issue receded in that
form, as if personality had at least as much to do with the
matter as denomination.

In Stages C and D we have had a mixed team, well-
balanced denominationally and rich in diversity of personality but there are some denominational themes of difference
which emerge from time to time:

(a) *The Establishment* – Although there have been moments
    when the 'wealth' of the Church of England felt like too
    much power, it impinges on the team less than the
    Anglican style of relationship where the community
    tends to be more supporting and less challenging of the
    structures. It is as if the Free Church team members are

particularly proud of the 'protest' tradition within their Protestantism.

(b) *The Church* – Historically Anglicans have had a commitment to parish ministry which tends to place less emphasis on the primary nature of the gathering of the committed Christians on a Sunday morning as if that is only one element in a range of Kingdom foci. For some Catholics it seems that attendance at Mass is the limit of their formal church involvement, so that they too are not working with a primary concept of developed congregational life.

(c) *Church Government* – Locally we all happily work with a judicious blend of decision-making by team, church council (and its sub-committees) and congregational meeting – although some Free Church members still feel that 'the church meeting' ought to be much stronger in the blend. Anglicans are inclined to look to the bishop for some approvals. This might on occasion be a grasp after roots or even a bit of gender assurance (while all bishops in England are male), but it feels more like the Anglican way of ensuring good connection between local and universal.

(d) *The People* – There is a recurring Free Church emphasis that it is the local people who matter and there would be a ready resistance to anything which seemed elitist. While some Anglicans might expect a carol service to imitate the choral excellence of a cathedral, those from other traditions might expect that for once everyone will know all the tunes and be able to join in heartily.

You only have to hint at some of the above tendencies to know that they are caricatures and that any generalisation is hardly far from denominational stereotyping. Again here personality seems to count for so much. But is there such a thing as an Anglican or Catholic or Free Church personality? Why are so many Anglicans indecisive? Why are so many Catholics uncompromising? Why are so many Free Church people protest-ant? Did they choose that denomination because they were so? It is possible that personality has been attracted to denomination in this way. For those who remain in the denomination in which they were brought up, could you say that their denomination has made them the kind of people they are? My experience makes me think that it is rather the case that they have simply found within their denominational range the stance which suits their personality.

PERSONALITY

One of the areas on which we have had to work as a mixed team has been not so much that of gender, as that of personality. It's been as if we've discovered who we are as individuals in relation to each other, that we have encountered both the times of conflict and the moments of growth.

What follows is a look at some of the areas in which the team has had differing responses to issues which might seem to have gender implications. These issues have been ones in which, in fact, we have divided more on personality (and denomination) than on gender.

Decision-making

Sometimes the view is expressed that men are more capable of decision-making than women. To caricature, men are the people who are outgoing, clear, capable of analysing the issues and making up their minds. On the other hands, women are indecisive, unclear, and take a long time to resolve issues.

The experience in our team has been that decision-making has gone more on the lines of personality than of gender. When it comes to the time for the team to make a decision about some matter, there have been varying views as to how this should be done. For example, if we are engaged in planning for the Christmas services, there are some in the team who would rather make up their minds on their own, others who feel the whole team should divide and a third view which says that decision-making is not within the remit of the team, but of the local Ecumenical Council of the church. Part of the dilemma in decision-making is the different denominational approaches – some team members have a more hierarchical view, others a more consensus approach, reflecting different denominational positions.

The differing views on the process of decision-making are reflected also in a different attitudes to decision-making on a personal basis. There are those in the team who are more enthusiastic about making decisions and others who would rather put this off until another day. It is probably one of the men who most likes to put decisions off, while one of the women most enjoys decision-making.

What we have felt to be important is that we cultivate a shared process of listening and discussing, honouring differing attitudes.

Leadership

Related to the question of decision-making is the matter of leadership. In traditional Christian understanding, leadership is a male domain. Biblical texts can be referred to, emphasising a male role in authority. The traditions of the church have largely emphasised a male role in leadership and it is these traditions which are still in the majority across the major churches today.

The experience of working in a mixed gender team has been that traditional male stereotypes of leadership have been altered.

Both men and women have been given the possibility of acting out of their different strengths, rather than conforming to a pre-determined pattern. The fact of working in an ecumenical team where there are differing understandings of leadership has actually led to a new openness about the possibility of sharing leadership in a variety of ways. The honouring of different strengths has meant that women have been accepted as, e.g. chairing meetings and undertaking the management and planning for the life of the church, while men have been free to develop gifts of creativity and gentleness. The different styles of leadership offered have depended more on the different personal characteristics of the team member involved.

Feeling and Thinking

At times there is a stereotyping which claims women to be feeling people and men to be thinking people. This means that women are automatically more suitable for roles such as pastoral care, and get put in that kind of pigeonhole. However, there is a question as to whether in the life of the church as a whole, there are more men than the national average who take on a feeling role, because of the kind of work and lifestyle portrayed by the church. In a recent Myers-Briggs Indicator Workshops, we discovered that two men and one woman in the team comes out as having an orientation towards feeling, and one man and one woman as having an orientation towards thinking.

Each member of the team is involved in pastoral care in different ways. However, due to the size of the congregation we have developed a network of lay pastoral care visitors who undertake the primary visiting of members of the congregation. It is interesting to note that pastoral care on a systematic basis is carried out by a team of lay pastoral care visitors, who are organised by the two 'thinking' members of the team!

Conflict

A further stereotyping that is sometimes made is that it is men who are more engaged in entering into conflict, whether in terms of causing conflict or of being unafraid of dealing with conflict. The experience in our team has been however that we have not divided between men and women in this area but rather on grounds of personality. Some team members, both male and female, are more inclined to address matters of disagreement openly as these arise; while other team members, both male and female, would rather work around such matters or concentrate on avoiding them.

Areas of conflict arise both over particular concrete proposals and over the ways in which people or difficult situation should be handled. The team has worked over the years on developing ways of handling conflict that leads neither to avoidance or over-robust argument. It has been important to share different insights from our different approaches in order to work on a common understanding. When we have been able to achieve this it has been possible to free much creative energy.

CONCLUSION

Developing Wholeness – The Coming Together Of The 'Masculine' And The 'Feminine'

Working in a mixed gender team has helped us to be set free from gender stereotypes in a way that has developed both the 'masculine' and the 'feminine' within the team and within each member of the team. I believe that working in such a way has freed more energy for the tasks in front of us. Learning to accept each other and help one another work on our strengths and weaknesses while at times a difficult process has brought its own rewards in terms of personal growth and development.

Working ecumenically and working with a team of different gender and personality gives us a pattern which is perceived by the congregation as life giving and creative. It gives us a model for community living which enlarges our understanding of the church. It is not always easy but it is a source of fulfilment.

6

Developing a reflective spirituality in management

NORMAN TODD

A consultant to senior managers remarked to me that part of
his work was to help them to pray in a totally secular way. By
this I assumed he did not mean an appeal to the unknown as
a last resort. Rather it was the ability to relax body, mind,
heart and will, in order to become aware of, and focus afresh
on, the supposed realities that confront them, and on their
responses to them.

Management

In order to manage we have to have an idea and an understanding of what we are managing, how it works and how it
is affected by outside agencies and its general environment.
The clearer and more accurate this idea and understanding,
the more effective becomes our management. Everyone
manages something whether it is a national economy or a
domestic kitchen, a medical practice or a new baby, an international conglomerate or a youth club, a diocese or a parish
church. We all know what is meant by the enquiry, 'How are
you managing?' or 'Can you manage?' whether addressed by
a director to a manager or a mother to her toddler.

It is as if, in order to manage, we have to have an internal
working model of what is 'out there'. If our model does not
correspond closely with outer reality then we are not living in
the real world, we are building castles in the air, we do not
have our feet on the ground. So this ability to form an effective working model of the particular part of the world we are

living in is of fundamental importance to us if we are going to manage at all. Indeed, a number of writers claim that this ability to reflect is fundamental to being a human person.

Reflecting

Carl Jung hailed it as 'the cultural instinct par excellence'. 'By way of the reflective instinct a stimulus becomes a psychic content and experience through which a natural automatic process may be transformed into a conscious creative one.' 'Without the reflecting consciousness of man the world is a gigantic meaningless machine, for as far as we know man is the only creature that can discover meaning.' And 'meaning is the quality ascribed to something which gives it value' (p. 128).

Not only can I form this inner image of my outer world; I can also form an image of my self, and of myself forming the image. 'Animals undergo evolutionary progress in which biologically determined response patterns are played out. History requires the capacity for self-reflection.' 'The subjective self could be thought of as represented by the self-reflexive "I am" in the sentence, "I am being attacked".' (Ogden pp. 49, 80)

Thus self-reflection uses the metaphor of a mirror reflecting (bending back) the light that falls upon it, but perceived as forming an image within it. The more even the surface of the glass and the more efficient the mercury on the back, then the more accurate the image will be. If, as is often suggested for meditation, we are more like a pool of water than a mirror, then, in order to reflect clearly and accurately, our surface has to be unruffled and our depths still.

T. S. Eliot, who combined the ability to reflect with that of being able to communicate his reflection, commended the type of reflective leisure described as follows. 'Leisure is a form of silence, of that silence which is the prerequisite of the apprehension of reality; only the silent hear and those who do not remain silent do not hear. Silence, as it is used in this context, does not mean "dumbness" or "noiselessness"; it means more nearly that the soul's power to "answer" to the reality of the world is left undisturbed. For leisure is a receptive attitude of mind, a contemplative attitude, and it is not only the occasion but also the capacity for steeping oneself in the whole of creation.' (in Pieper p. 52)

Reflection has been described at some length. Here are shorter descriptions of the ways in which other words in the title are used.

Spirituality

Spirit is the nexus of values, meaning and non-material essence of anything. It is not a special kind of very rarefied matter. The material and the spiritual are two distinct, though not therefore unconnected, ways in which we experience ourselves and everything else. Spirit is not a thing. It is the principle of unity, the non-material reality from which radiate what we experience as pointing back to its source (i.e. value, meaning, essence, wholeness).

Spirituality is the pattern of exercises and habits of body, mind, feeling and spirit by which we maintain and grow our spirit and become aware of spirit about us.

Although I have emphasised that we all have to manage in the sense of 'cope as effectively as possible', we must also consider particularly those men and women whose work is managing an organisation whether it is secular or religious. In both we have to guard against idolatry, that is valuing our internal working model rather than the reality which it – inevitably inadequately – represents. Every model is provisional and has to be continually updated because the outer reality is changing and because our ability to reflect will vary. Sometimes there will be big changes and our internal model will become increasingly inadequate, the dissonance manifesting as anxiety. In a time such as ours of chaotic change there will be considerable anxiety; we feel lost because we have lost our bearings between our internal and external worlds. We feel we have lost meaning, values, unity: lost spirit. Our spirituality (exercises and habits) has let us down, either because we have neglected it, or because it needs reconstructing.

Change

The working models are personal adaptations of those which are shared by others in our culture, both our general culture and the specific culture of the organisation in which we manage. They are not just ideas, cognitive models; they include emotional attitudes and whatever comes through all the receptors we possess. (e.g. Jung's thinking, feeling, sensing, intuiting, each in introvert or extrovert form). Such shared internal reflections of outer realities also change, usually slowly but sometimes with revolutionary suddenness.

The classic example of the sudden total change (paradigm change) is the abandonment of the phlogiston theory by the scientific establishment. In industry there have been shifts in the use of power. A smaller example is given by Deming (pp. 9, 10) of a firm which stuck with manufacturing carburettors and was out of business when cars switched to fuel injectors.

The gradual change and the paradigm shift also occur in religions. The Bible is full of them; for example, Abraham discovering that human sacrifice was not what was required by his God. Those who manage in religious organisations have to cope with anxiety and unease, though perhaps in a more intense form for it is to do with ultimate concern. Theological odium is notorious. A comparison between science and theology is made by Capra in 'Belonging to the Universe'. 'The metaphors of the Bible point towards religious truth, but they are not the full truth. So the metaphor should not be confused with the truth towards which the metaphor points.' (p. 39)

Practise

So we need a reflective and self-reflective spirituality. How can we develop and keep fresh this ever-responsive pattern of exercises and habits? A musician has to practise scales in order to practise music. To practise medicine a doctor has to learn and practise healing skills and attitudes. How can we practise – develop – reflective spirit in order for it to become part of us?

Relaxation

We must make time for leisure in the sense approved by T. S. Eliot and quoted above. First we have to learn to relax our body. People relax for childbirth, for sport, for singing, for acting. Most methods use the technique of first tensing a part of the body and then letting it relax, moving round until the whole body is relaxed. Then there is further relaxation linked with breathing. I liken it to going down a ratchet; each time I breathe out I relax my whole body down another notch and stay there while I breathe in, then sink another notch with the next exhalation.

With our body relaxed we relax our mind. Again there are various methods. I find the best is to relax my eyes. Not the facial muscles round the eyes, they are already relaxed, but the actual eyeballs. Usually our eyes are darting hither and thither and our thoughts with them. In normal life this may be necessary, though not with the anxiety often present. It takes time to learn how to relax in this way. As the eyes relax, so do the thoughts. Once the 'monkey chatter' of preoccupied thought subsides a different kind of thought rises up, as it were, from the depths. It is slow, almost playful. 'The still small voice of calm.' It is worth listening to. We are like a child wondering at new discovery. It is the beginning of meditation; thought seemingly given rather then driven or maintained by us.

Such exercises are best done in outward quiet at least until we are adept. Then we can reach a point at which the inward quiet drowns the outward noise. Usually, too, it is best to have our eyes closed. Now, still relaxed, comes the time to open them. We move about very slowly noticing how our body works, enjoying the balance and the way we are part of it and it is part of us. We learn to walk in meditation.

Contemplation

Then we begin noticing what is about us, looking at it without discursive thought. Look at anything, small or large as if it is the first time we have seen it. Just being a mirror or a pool reflecting internally whatever we are looking at. We

find that our other senses also become more receptive and
that we are aware of them. This is the beginning of contem-
plation. We can look inwards as well as outwards and reflect
something of the mystery of our inner being, though for most
of us it takes time to learn. We are beginning to reflect our
self as it reflects.

For most of us it may be necessary to have a course of such
exercises on a weekend retreat or a series of shorter periods.
Then we have to practise regularly, most would say, daily.
Regular frequency is more important then long periods. We
aim, not to eliminate normal discursive thought in favour of
reflection, but to be able to choose which is appropriate and
to enter into it.

Sharing together

The development of a corporate spirituality in a team,
company or church is analogous to that in a single person.
However, it seems that some kind of team or group has
to mediate between the person and the larger organisation. It makes sense to speak of the spirit of a company
whether it be of twelve or of twelve thousands; the esprit
de corps; the quality of sharing bread together (the etymol-
ogy of 'company'). As with a single person we can examine
the nexus of values, meaning, non-material essence and
principle of unity. We do it by reflecting together, sharing
our reflections, learning a pattern of corporate exercises
and corporate habits; developing a corporate reflective
spirituality.

There are ways of eliciting from people how they construct
internal reflections of the spirit of the various grouping and
organisations to which they belong or have belonged or
would like to belong. From these a corporate reflection can
be constructed – a kind of photo-fit. When a company is in
good spiritual health it will be able to form this realistic,
always fresh, reflection of its self interacting with its environment. It will not get stuck with yesterday's unrevised
reflections, nor remain stuck with only one model or
metaphor when more are required to cope with the complexities of its life.

Development

There is not space in a short chapter to describe the methods which can help us develop reflective spirit. We can all learn from the pioneers of spirit in religious and secular traditions. The parables of Jesus are all invitations to reflect and they create a space for us to revise, or revolutionise our working reflections. Religious communities, management consultants, organisation studies can all contribute, though not all may use the language of spirit. The parallels between secular appraisal and spiritual discipline are fruitful. Perhaps confession does not figure in either as prominently as it should.

In religious companies the language of spirit is explicit. This does not necessarily mean that it is more healthy than the implicit language of spirit in a secular company, merely that its state of health or sickness is more immediately obvious. 'Judgement is seen to begin at the household of God.'

It may be thought that reflective spirituality is a method of development which is neutral; that it can be used for ill or for good, to pollute or to make whole. I suggest that this is not so. To tangle with spirit is to tangle with something greater than human nature and human company. It is to allow some kind of contact with the mystery which in the Christian tradition is called 'Holy Spirit of God'.

If management consultancy does have something to do with a secular form of prayer, may I conclude by using a prayer of St Paul for me and for you. 'Since the day we heard about you, we have not stopped praying for you and asking God to fill you with the knowledge of his will through all spiritual wisdom and understanding.'

REFERENCES

Capra, F. et al. Belonging to the Universe (Penguin, 1992).

Deming, W. E., The New Economics (Massachusetts IT, 1993).

Jung, C. G. in Samuels A Critical Dictionary of Jungian Analysis (R & KP, 1986).

Ogden, T. H. The Matrix of the Mind (Maresfield Lib, 1992).

Pieper, J. Leisure the Basis of Culture (Faber & Faber, 1952).

7

Towards redefining the role of ministry

CATHERINE M. RYAN

My work often brings me into direct contact with priests at the grass roots, both individually and collectively. One recent occasion was a 'Futures Planning' workshop in which the sixty-six clergy of the Eastern Pastoral Area of the Roman Catholic Diocese of Westminster participated. The format replaced that of the traditional 'Bishop and Priests Away Week' held every eighteen months, and was a breakthrough. For the first time, the clergy had publicly recognised that the face of the Catholic Church in the four London Boroughs of Hackney, Tower Hamlets, Camden and Islington[1] was changing in such a way that crisis was inevitable unless they acted collegially to formulate a vision of a desired future, and then co-operated with one another to bring it to reality.

The collegial flavour of the workshop was itself novel: in the day-to-day situation, diocesan clergy rarely have the opportunity to work together across parishes; additionally, the usual patter of the 'Away Week' was that after consultation, a topic was selected, a speaker engaged, and a schedule of lectures and discussions arranged. Attendance at either of the two parallel 'Away Weeks' had been the norm, and it was unofficially recognised that straight input sessions predominated. This year, however was different. It was seen to be so important that the matter of 'Futures Planning' was addressed that everyone agreed to attend together – a first. The level of commitment to task and the energy generated was high, at least in part because clergy were aware of

91

an uncertain future looming, and wanted some sense of soli-
darity in approaching it.

Early on, it was recognised that the absence of other
church members and the lack of previous consultation about
their desired future as local church, would necessitate action
to be taken in the parishes to make up the deficiency. Each
priest agreed that ways would be sought in the succeeding
months, for people to partake in similar exercises, designed
to suit the needs of the particular parish. Additionally, repre-
sentatives from each parish would congregate a year later to
share vision and progress, and plan for the next year's work.

Defining leadership

Mid-way through the time of the workshop, the ten small
working groups were sharing five-year goals within the
assembly. Members of one group had detailed the kind of
leadership they wanted to see. They wanted to work
towards:

> the greater use of, and development of, resources and training
> for ongoing formation of catechists, leaders and priests ...
> Priests and leaders to be fully aware of and sensitive to differ-
> ent cultures within the community.[2]

Discussing the feedback, a tangle sense of unease emerged
around the word 'leader'. What was the role of the leader,
and who would these leaders be? Some said that clergy
should not *automatically* take the leadership role; others felt
that clergy should *never* take the leadership role in local
church. Still others thought that *only* the priest could and
should play the role of leader within the parish community.
Eventually, one of the youngest participants commented: 'I
don't see anyone not wanting actively to exercise their priesthood in the 1990s and beyond, but I *do* see an uncertainty
about what that role is for today'. Obviously he had hit the
nail on the head, for the relief was evident, and energy once
more buzzed around the room.[3] Who were they as priests,
now, in the 1990s? The role they had been trained to fulfil
now seemed inappropriate, and no obvious and authorised
alternative had emerged to fill its place. For these clergy,

however, the 'Aha!' moment generated realisation without diminishing the anxiety; they were unable to follow through and address the uncertainty. Soon the conversation had moved on and they were addressing less threatening matters, with simpler solutions, such as catechesis. For me, this is one 'prong' of the forces which often result in a clerical inertia in the churches and stifle wider involvement: even when blocks can be identified, addressing the source of the block may prove too painful and the situation becomes even more intractable.

Structure of administration

Another 'prong' springs from the effects of working in a hierarchy which is at the same time a bureaucracy. The Early Church, the model to which we often aspire, was an *ad hoc* organic structure, at least in part due to the early stage in its development, which facilitated, in current terminology, a predisposition to organisational learning[4] and the ability to be highly responsive to environmental conditions. Growth in size and geographical spread meant the adoption of formal structures, standardisation and the accompanying bureaucracy which now characterises all our churches. This is critical when considering the effects of, and the need to escape from, clericalism, since bureaucracies can have a debilitating effect on people involved.

Relationships in the hierarchy/bureaucracy mean that the majority of clergy fall in the middle, with diocesan administrations 'above' and lay people 'below'. Thus sandwiched and answerable to both groups, these clergy experience a particular range of difficulties which compound the effects of clericalism and complicate attempts to leave it behind. Sometimes the problems result from the necessity of strategic planning, as in the case of the clergy cited at the beginning of this chapter. If, for example, diocesan administrations know that medium/long-term strategic planning is necessary in response to present social and demographic trends, but hesitate to make the necessary decisions, either for fear of hurting someone, or because of anxiety that the trend may one day be reversed while changes, once made, cannot, clergy can feel that there is 'fudging' going on over which they have no control. This leads to frustration as parishioners cannot be consulted and worked with towards necessary changes, and plans cannot be made and implemented at local level because of procrastination at diocesan level. Clergy are in an ambiguous situation because they are unable to act as they see fit. Decisions may eventually be made but only when a crisis point has been reached. Now any decision appears brutal and it is certainly unheralded; what is more the same clergy are expected to pick up the pieces on the ground and uphold the official line. The management literature yields some comment on such situations:

> Under these conditions, administrators often appear to be powerful and authoritative, but also ambiguous, unknowable, and arbitrary. Workers come to believe that their performances will inevitably be found inadequate in unpredictable ways – that shame is a certain result of any effort. Shame anxiety interferes with a realistic assessment of organisational authority and keeps subordinates from learning how to assume sufficient authority to define and execute their own responsibilities.[5]

Whilst this type of situation may not be mirrored exactly throughout the denominations, there are parallels, direct and indirect.[6] My contention is that clergy, for a multitude of reasons, have frequently been left in a situation sufficiently ambiguous to cause real personal anxiety and difficulties in relating to authority, which lead to taking defensive action. That defensive action may, in fact, result in an entrenchment of clericalism as the clergy turn in on themselves or further resist attempts to introduce new ways of ministering. If it proves impossible to maintain a sense of self-preservation by doing this, some are taking alternative action and resigning their priesthood. It seems that this course of action is becoming more common and while reasons for this are doubtless more complex than simply frustration within the system,[7] they make an important contribution to an individual's self-perception and their need to take defensive action of one sort or another.

When clergy advance in the system, as in any other, it is

difficult to avoid playing out old tapes, and continuing dysfunctional patterns in new situations and over long periods of time. When this continues, I believe that in addition to individuals perpetuating such patterns, there comes ultimately to be built into the system a self-generating momentum which has the same effect.[8] Since it acts at an unconscious level, it is all the more difficult to identify and address, and is therefore a vicious circle.

Church members, too, grow up with an expectation of the ordained ministry and of their own role in the church which colludes with the difficulties outlined above. Some are not happy with what they see and actively seek to bring about changes; others, never having known anything else, are happy to follow the crowd as passive attenders. Understanding and accepting a personal calling within the church is frequently an unfamiliar concept. Only the very few, I feel, are in a situation where they are able actively to exercise their own ministry within the body.[9]

Re-energising the system

And so to look towards action. If we are even to aspire to the model of church portrayed in the Acts of the Apostles, but inserted into the twentieth and twenty-first centuries, how can we address the stranglehold of clericalism so that the churches can be energised truly to reclaim the 'priesthood of all believers'?

First, and most crucial, action needs to be multi-level: clericalism cannot be reduced, let alone eradicated, unless each layer of the system co-operates to this end. So, work in diocesan administrations must be accompanied by work with church members, as well as the main body of clergy and those wishing to join their number. In each case what needs to be done will be different.

Diocesan administrations must review their strategic (and other) action to assess how they contribute to the prolongation of clericalism within the churches. Is the 'espoused theory' the same as the 'theory in action'?[10] Does the way things work, allow the main body of clergy to fulfil their ministry with the maximum of support and the minimum of internal contradictions? Is it best for many of the senior administrative posts to be held by clergy?[11] Are there not highly qualified people around who can do these jobs and so begin to break the clerical strangehold? At diocesan level, are clergy appointments the managerial responsibility of clerics? Is there a need to keep things in clerical hands, or are we not simply perpetuating the system by so doing? After all, in the early church, even bishops were appointed from among the faithful to be shepherd of that flock. They did not have to be ordained already!

For most of the clergy, those with parochial responsibility, I would consider two things. Is there a value to be had in changing the pattern of pastoral ministry, so that old perceptions begin to break down? Peter Cornwell, in his 1995 Lenten lecture at St James', Piccadilly,[12] distinguished between the Anglican priesthood as a profession and the Roman Catholic priesthood as a craft. Students at Roehampton Institute London,[13] considering the same point, concluded that priesthood in all the major traditions, had once been characterised by a time when enthusiasm was equivalent to expertise, but that at varying speeds, there was a trend away from this towards specialism. This had both positive and negative features. My experience of clergy tells me that, in the 1990s, it is rare to find a priest who is completely happy in the *Curé d'Ars* model, and that every ordained minister should have the opportunity to practise pastoral ministry alongside some kind of specialist ministry. This latter builds self-esteem and generates energy for the priest, which spills over into the rest of the ministry. I am convinced this is a positive way forward which should be considered in every mainstream church if not already being considered. Another way of achieving this may be to examine whether the 'worker-priest' or NSM model has any positive contribution to make on this score. Both of these approaches, it seems to me, could potentially turn on their heads, problems with lack of personnel to carry out the necessary pastoral ministry, for they may both prompt more lay people to become actively involved in their churches, and enable clergy to gain energy in other spheres which can free them for their pastoral ministry.

Priesthood of all believers

But perhaps for me the most important, and underpinning, action would be steps to reclaim the priesthood of all believers, for all believers. This does not mean an undermining of the ministerial priesthood, but a relocating of what it means to be ordained within the concept of the priesthood of all. I have been on the receiving end of grand plans, initiated by those with time to think them up but not required to implement them; this is not what I mean. I mean reflective action more low-key than that: to engage in a common reflection on what it means to be called by God, at every level in the church, and with all simplicity, open to receive from one another without 'rank'. This will require a degree of vulnerability from the ordained minister, and no hiding behind roles. But it will enhance the quality of relationship and lay the foundations for a new way of being church.

NOTES

1. The four boroughs of which the Pastoral Area is comprised.
2. Proceedings of Eastern Area Bishop and Priests 'Away Week' 1995, p. 3.
3. Groups reaching such a sticking-point are usually grappling with something unidentified which is blocking their forward movement. If this can be identified it is usually sufficient to free energy, which of itself provides the necessary impetus for change. Such a realisation can be called an 'Aha!' moment.
4. Work on organisational life cycles indicates that organisations which begin life in an *ad hoc* manner may learn more from initial performance feedback (so-called *enactive* learning) and respond to environmental conditions more easily than those which are highly structured from the start (these organisations are said to learn *proactively*). As time proceeds, however, the operations of enactive organisations are likely to crystallise into a pattern which means they are less likely to respond to environmental changes. See, for example, the work of Miles and Randolph in Kimberly, J., Miles, R. and Associates, 1980, *The Organisational Life Cycle* (San Francisco: Jossey Bass).
5. Baum, Howell S., 1991, 'How Bureaucracy Discourages Responsibility', in M. F. R. Kets de Vries (ed.), *Organisations on the Couch: Clinical Perspectives on Organisational Behaviour and Change* (San Francisco: Jossey Bass).
6. An example from my own consultancy experience was with a group of Anglican PCCs, involved in a change from parochial to team

ministry. They had been working in an interim, 'group ministry' situation, for a number of years but the pastoral measure had not been finalised in order to legalise the change the PCCs wanted. There seemed to be a conflict of interest between what was felt necessary at grass roots level and what the relevant authorities perceived as being possible. In fact it seemed, on the receiving end, to be merely that such a combination of features had not been combined in a Team Ministry Pastoral Measure within the jurisdiction.

Indirect parallels in all denominations may hinge around a relational change between clergy and their immediate hierarchy: superiors are now more pastorally involved with their clergy than in earlier times. A role confusion can result, with blurring between that of legitimate superior to priest, and of pastoral carer to person who is also a 'subordinate'. The nature and role of authority may be correspondingly unclear, if the relationship is accompanied by elements of pastoral care for priest and family. How can fair boundaries be drawn between administration and pastoral care? Has human resources management anything to teach us on this?

7. Lack of permanence as a characteristic of Western society in the late twentieth century, and the complex web of causal factors impinges on the ability and perceived desirability of permanent commitment within the ministry.

8. Stories of 'When I was a young priest' are legion, and every minister has their own horror stories.

9. c.f. 1 Corinthians 12: 12–26.

10. See Argyris and Schön (1978); *Organisational Learning: A Theory of Action Perspective* (Addison Wesley). These authors distinguish between an organisation's 'espoused theory' (what it states it adheres to) and its 'theory in action' (what is observable in the public arena) – a sort of organisation 'do as I say, don't do as I do'. Failure to recognise any distinction is often a major cause of stress and can lead to disillusionment with public bodies and organisations. It is also the opposite of St Paul's advice in Philippians 4:9 'Keep on doing the things that you have learned and received and heard and seen in me, and the God of peace will be with you.'

11. I notice with great sadness that declining finances (in all the mainstream churches) and increasing clerical anxiety (at least in some of the mainstream churches) are bringing about an increase in vacant posts being filled by clergy – or in some cases, not being filled at all. I cannot believe that in every case, despite what is published, the reasons focus on changing needs within the diocese or within the church (e.g. 'We have no need of Adult Educators in this area in the 1990s').

12. See the edited version of the lecture in *The Tablet*; Vol. 249, issue 8069, p. 417–419.

13. Postgraduate Diploma in Management for Ministry, Year One, Ministry Management Module.

8

Understanding new patterns of management in ministry

ROBIN GREENWOOD

What is it that we do to people at ordination? Where do the attitudes, mannerisms and expectations come from? Every human organisation has its particular games – the National Trust, the T.U.C., the House of Commons, the secondary school, the courts, and the churches. In all of them there are hierarchies of power, salary, information, and influence which sometimes take on bizarre outworkings: who has which space in the car park, what proportion of a secretary's time is my due, what level of furnishing is appropriate at my level of seniority, or what is the ceiling for my personal expenses? It would be strange if church leaders and administrators were free of such foibles and yet we cannot just leave it there for churches lay claim to announcing their aims through their internal life and external communication.

A Long Period of Transition

My own quarter of a century of ordained ministry has coincided with a time of new hopes for the churches, radical changes in expectation of the role and function of clergy and laity as well as a massive resistance. To the general public churches are a mystery – what do they represent? In 1970, after a long summer of working 12 hour shifts at a brewery, ordination propelled me into a church culture maintained by predominantly elderly and confident clergymen. There was the unwordly scholar who followed his training of the 1920s in which the morning was for the study (really studying, yes even the New Testament in Greek) and the afternoon for visiting women and the elderly; there was the noisy and fast-moving cleric who spent a week each month typing the parish magazine and whose conversation seemed limited to the latest mistakes of the Archdeacon; and there was the smiling, eager priest (with three young children and devoted but weary wife) who spent every waking hour devising and running services, caring and teaching programmes for all ages, and taking funerals. Congregations in the 1970s were those who, on the whole, were expecting to be dependent on a godly man set apart who was given to them by the Bishop, and with whom you had to deal on his terms. One influential senior priest I can recall from my curacy days assumed the goodwill of everyone, chose to spend a great deal of time preparing long and convoluted Church Council speeches to read to exhausted businessmen and elderly women always with the expectation that this judgement was right, and with a take-it-or-leave-it attitude about whether parishioners came to church or not. Although this remoteness and lack of awareness was often accompanied by a fear of intimacy, positively I observed a real devotion to saying the office, cele-brating the eucharist, retreats, reading and time-consuming care for those in human crisis or seeking rites of passage.

In researching my book *Transforming Priesthood* (1994) I collected together evidence of the clergy formation in the first half of the present century. From written evidence (theology, manuals of practice, and biographies) the picture that emerged of a Church of England security rooted in the domi-nant role of the clergy had the following elements:

Myths of Christian origins

The prevailing ecclesiology represented classically by R. C. Moberley's *Ministerial Priesthood* (reprinted as a textbook throughout the first half of the century) limited 'the ministry' to bishops, priests and deacons by a carefully selective read-ing of the New Testament and pre-Nicine periods. The policy of the Church of England was declared to be the true inheritance of the early church and the ministerial arrangements could therefore be regarded as the guarantee of Anglican authority. There were challenges from the prophetic voices of Ramsey, Allen, Barry, Robinson, Gibbs and others, but only with the ecumenical international debate of the 1980s (Küng, Schillebeeckx, L. Boff, Suenens, Möltmann, Zizioulas and many others) has the excitement of a new way of understanding what it is to be 'church' received wide acceptance. Robert Warren's *Building Missionary Congregations* (1994), represents the degree of movement away from clericalism in the Church of England which is now taking place.

Manuals of practice

Second-hand shops contain collections of charges and lectures by those who taught ordinands in the period 1900–1960 – many of whom later became bishops. Common elements are the expectation that clergy are chiefly pastors, they are in sole charge, with lay help carefully controlled, the clergy will work an exacting day and are directly and clearly answerable to God. What hope then of challenging such a vocation? What parishioner could question the decision of one in daily touch with heaven? What hope for a wife and family to compete for the vicar's time – against God himself! What right has such a priest to care for his own life? No wonder vocation leaflets were often dominated by representations of Christ on the cross – the model for the long-suffering minister who represented God to God's people. Biographies and parish histories reinforce this picture of the clergyman who 'takes leave' occasionally but is on duty night and day by divine appointment. There was glorious devotion, spirituality, integrity, fulfilment and many good fruits but at what awesome cost! How much limitation to human development, not to mention damage to marriage and parent-child relationships and to the dignity of the laity cannot be calculated.

Sole charge

The introvert, thinker, sensitive male 'not as other men' recruited for parish ministry, entered into a collusion of being omnicompotent and above challenge, the product and victim of a culture encouraged by dependent laity. The love-hate relationship with 'professionalism' and having 'a career' amongst the clergy is still around today. Bishops and Archdeacons see there is apparently a bottomless need for clergy to be cared for, to having their abilities recognised, and be acknowledged as highly competent. Frustratingly they are all too often in competition with each other and other churches, find team work hard and often seem to prefer a reputation for over work rather than for being strategists and in touch with tranquility. In the local church insecure leadership, poor self-esteem and boundary keeping often results in jealousy about territory and decision-making. It does little for building up the confidence of the laity and is one of the reasons why many wise people absent themselves from church because it does not sustain them or serve the wider community.

Holy Management in the Local Church

The agenda which I believe churches need to work at today is enabled and informed by a cluster of elements which span theoretical and practical disciplines: theology, organisational theory, psychology, spirituality, and economics. There is a widespread consensus today that churches are not to be defined in terms of a guaranteed clerical ministry.

Essentially what makes a church is its willingness to become an instrument of God's own mission to bring wholeness to all creation. The church in every local place, and together globally, has no other legitimate purpose except to be an agent of the kingdom values lived and explicated by Jesus Christ. There is no room for games of power, dependency and denial – its about letting God bring about maturing and healthy relationship. Its total membership is its task force – in the workplace, community, home, institutions, and movements for ethical and social reform. Its way of life is its lived gospel proclamation. Its ministerial arrangements and management of people, for better or worse, cannot hide its beliefs. The way its inner (sacraments, word communal) networks of relationships relate to its dispersed (evangelical, caring, challenging, justice-seeing) endeavours tells the truth about its capacity to serve God's mission. Jesus' invitation is concerned with the challenge for disciplines to grow up into their rightful vocation as God's people and to work for the maturity and final destiny (*Shalom*) of the whole created order.

It is vital, therefore, that the clerical leadership of this eschatological movement – the church – is healthy, self-aware and strong enough to be of use *in this particular task*. Pressures of finance and projected numbers of clergy are not the only factors to form future diocesan policies. Learning from systems thinking we can identify whole clusters of integrated issues.

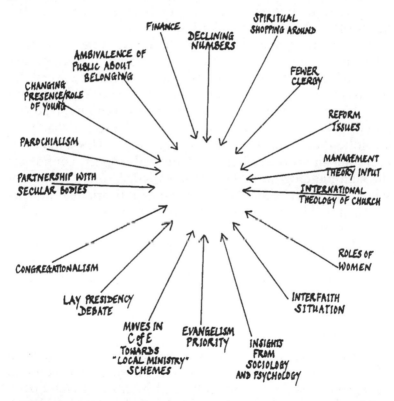

When pressure is brought to bear on one part of an organisation there will be changes all round and attempted solutions will need to take account of as many aspects as possible.

A growing concern for discipleship

The Turnbull Commission Report (1995) invites the Church to share a common insight today in organisational theory of becoming a 'learning organisation'.[1] Having spent so long with the delusion that the Church has only to speak and people will listen, there is now a challenge to recognise that it is often precisely by showing ourselves ready to listen and learn that we command most respect and in intangible ways, by so doing, help those who speak to come to fresh insights of their own. This more fragile and yet confident image and process of generating constant improvement needs to be modelled by clergy and all church members in their particular spheres of influence. It takes maturity to recognise the limits of our knowledge and ability.

A learning organisation, rather than working at reactive problem solving, fosters radical questioning, review, receiving outside information and feed-back. Instead of adversarial polarization between 'experts' and 'ignorant', clergy and laity, bishops and priests, theologians and accountants, doers and thinkers, pioneer and administrator, the spiritual and the worldly, there will be a dynamic tension.[2] This implies in everyone an attitude of enquiry, mutual respect, confidence through building up a body of knowledge, and a culture in which whoever should lead most appropriately at this moment will be free to do so and will be heard.

It goes without saying that a concern for discipleship in the church means that every Christian person – not an elite – will be offered good quality opportunities for the development of their faith, respecting their doubts, and for making connection with daily responsibilities.

A holistic rationality

The clergy we need now will be self-aware enough to recognise the inevitable limitedness of their own context, background, skills and attitudes and humble enough not to inflict them as the only authority on would-be church members. We can agonise about evangelism and a refusal of the public to come to church, but unless we can make a psychological space for a kaleidoscope of people and help dominant groups to recognise their own limited outlook, church membership will in reality not be open to the public. The ways in which we have rejected others, usually unconsciously, in the past should fill us with shame but still not let us off the hook of working with hope for future openness. Struggles to integrate order and spontaneity, Anglican form with pentecostal exuberance, evangelism and social concern, stability with work for justice, children and adults, women and men, volunteers with professionals, are all healthy signs of growth. Conflict in church meetings – rather than something to be feared and controlled – is part of having commitment. It shows that somebody cares passionately.

Feelings and intellect, planning and coping with the unexpected, all need to be integrated with the sense that churches are not talking to themselves but are essentially agents of communication and instruments of change in society. Fashions in management, followed too late by churches, have given this approach a poor press amongst some clergy, but there is wisdom to be integrated when church and bank agree that the careful management of people – in all their wonderful variety – is the key to success in institutional working out of 'mission'. Senior church 'managers' have a lot of learning to do when they still rejoice to be seen as over-busy, stressed, dabbling in too many committee meetings and concerns instead of making priorities and listening to their bodies and feelings as well as their heads.

A shared vision

So many churches are restricted by the theology which they espouse and the agendas of clergy who come and go. John Robinson wrote very accurately, 'No parish can ever get more excited than the vicar'. Others have recognized that certain clergy and laity in a church will be 'gatekeepers', either pulling others in to membership or the reverse, by their attitudes and actions towards others.

Recent international debate about the mission of churches draws attention to the trinitarian life of Godself.[3] Orthodox Christian belief holds that Father, Son and Spirit are both three and one simultaneously. The unique particularlity of

each Person of God is in balance with the fact that their identity flows from the relationship of mutuality that lies
between them. So God is a community of interactive love
overflowing into creation and inviting our response. Part of
the church's response is to emulate in its ministerial *koinonia*
patterns which the New Testament initiates and later prayer
and reflection has developed. A Christian community, called
to be a sign and foretaste of God's final dream for all
creation, will practise already – and fail frequently – the
mutual interrelatedness which characterises God. Within the
tension between locally expressed need and international
ecclesiological vision, churches have the task of devising their
particular contextualized agenda which is more than a list of
what the clergy alone are advocating.[4]

Ecumenical theology (Vatican 2, Lima, Porvoo) stresses
that it is baptism rather than ordination which gives access to
and creates the church's life. All ministries are of equal value
if different, all local churches have an equal place in the
scheme of things but are wild variations on the original
theme: Jesus and his first disciples, most typically in the
upper room. Churches can learn from the insights of modern
management regarding the ways in which ideas are created
together and how everyone becomes committed if a
common wish is articulated and revised as needed.[5]
Churches have all the theological authority needed to work
towards being communities where the voice is heard and
every contribution acknowledged. One of the roles of the
clergy is to find ways of discussing – in company with others
– what is God's requirement of *this* community, in *this* place,
at *this* particular time.

Team Learning

A church that is struggling to move beyond clericalism will
be fostering a sense of collaboration in which everyone is
learning together – as a constant attitude of mind.[6] No one
will regard themselves as dispensable, working in isolation,
or as having nothing to contribute to the progress of the local
church. All accredited ministers will see their education and
training as a life-long commitment. Churches and their

leadership team will recognise that the discerning of appropriate strategies for the church's mission will be a permanent
process of interactive, honest and often painful learning.

Churches can learn from 1990s management theories that
a sense of dignity and hope comes best where teams are
determined to be lean, fit, flexible, productive and cross-
functional. So everyone becomes more empowered and has
the opportunity to develop their full potential.[7]

Seeing the whole, being catholic

Organisational theory and system thinking, together with a
social trinitarian doctrine of God, indicate a way of being
church which requires clergy to restrain from simply getting
on with their 'own' work – however they choose to interpret
it. In a collaborative church clergy need to be people of
vision, able to help a community work out its policies or its
vocation. They will need to distinguish their own contribution from that of the whole church so that agreed aims can be
implemented. For this clergy need organisational skills –
negotiating, communicating, delegating, decision-making by
consensus, setting priorities, discerning when to be directive
or non-directive. Personally they must learn how to balance
time between work and leisure, know and keep appropriate
boundaries, and be able to serve without needing to be the
centre of attention or of receiving any positive affirmation
from others whatever the circumstances. Finally, it is the role
of the clergy in particular to accept the loneliness of living
some of the time on the boundaries between one local church
and another, the local and the universal, and the church and
wider society.

Conclusion

Many clergy are today being persuaded to recognise the need
to reframe their understanding of what is required of them.
In the new context of a church which defines itself more by
baptism than by ordination, clergy have a vital role as those
called to manage change as a continuing process.[8] They are
to ensure that all the resources of Christian faith and human
endeavour are directed to developing a vision and sense of

direction which can be owned by the whole church. Skills of communication, inspiring, and drawing out the genius of others will be primary. Good leadership requires an inner confidence in the ordained ministery so that he or she is in touch with their own feelings and with those with whom they deal. An ability to observe the responses of other people and to decide what response to make is an essential ingredient for ministerial practice.[9] Churches now require – not clerics who (however efficiently and devotedly) go it alone – those who know how to be (and encourage others to be) leaders and managers of the local church.[10] In themselves and others they must learn to engage the heart as well as the mind in binding together a group with a common concern to see in their often mundane routines the early signs of God's Kingdom.

NOTES

1. Peter M. Senge, *The Fifth Discipline* (Century Business, London, 1990).

2. Peter M. Senge, 'The Leader's Next Work: Building learning organisations', *Sloan Management Review*, Fall 1990, MIT Sloan School of Management.

3. Kevin Giles, *What on Earth is the Church?* (SPCK, 1995) and R. P. Greenwood, *Transforming Priesthood* (SPCK, 1994).

4. S. R. Covey, *The Seven Habits of Highly Effective People* (Simon and Shuster, London 1992).

5. Peter Brierley, *Vision Building: Knowing Where you are Going* (Hodder and Stoughton, London 1989).

6. T. Downs, *The Parish as Learning Community* (Paulist Press, New York 1979).

7. Phil Lowe and Ralph Lewis, *Management Development Beyond the Fringe* (Kogen Page, 1994).

8. M. Beer, R. A. Eisenstat, and B. Spector, 'Why Change Programs Don't Produce Change', Harvard Business Review, Nov-Dec 1990, pp. 158–166.

9. *Action Information*, Alban Institute, Washington DC, Vol. xviii, 2.

10. Covey describes the complementary tasks of management and leadership as 'two creations', see Note 4 above.

PART TWO

AGENDA FOR ORGANISATION

9

The church as a voluntary non-profit organisation

CHRIS BEMROSE

Management is not always held in high regard within the Church. Too often, it is seen in terms of orders and controls – stifling the creative spirit, rather than being about leadership and support. Will the increased focus on managerialism so evident in other sectors lead to bishops becoming like chief executives, priests like parish managers?

This article looks at some of the lessons from the voluntary sector in managing organisations with a strong sense of mission. It starts by enumerating some of the similarities between church and voluntary sector management, before exploring three general implications for church management. It concludes with a brief summary of the central distinctiveness between the church and other voluntary organisations.

Similarities in management issues

The history of church and charity is like two strands of rope, closely coupled through the centuries. The twelve disciples can be seen as a voluntary group, committed to a common cause: 'to preach the kingdom of God and to heal the sick' (Luke 9.2). They shared many characteristics of today's charities. They relied on voluntary donations and support (Luke 9.5), needed a trustworthy accountant (Luke 22.5), had internal disputes about status and position (Luke 9.46) and experienced sudden falls in membership (John 6.67).

Jesus' call to feed the hungry, to welcome strangers, to

look after the sick and to visit those in prison (Matthew 25.35–36) can be seen as a call to voluntary activity. With the word 'charity' derived from the Latin 'caritas', meaning Christian love of our fellow beings, it is not surprising that many of today's charities were inspired by Christians – the Samaritans, Relate (National Marriage Guidance) and Barnados to name just three.

The purposes of church and charity have some similarities. Drucker, in *Managing The Non-Profit Organisation* (1990), sees the product of a non-profit organisation as being 'a changed human being' – a purpose which is central for most religious organisations.

The characteristics of management also have parallels in both fields. In his book *Managing Without Profit: The Art of Managing Third Sector Organisations* (1995), Mike Hudson points to seven characteristics of non-profit organisations which make management particularly challenging. These include:

- Objectives which are difficult to define precisely: resulting in a temptation to adopt fuzzy objectives which do not provide a good basis for effective management;
- Performance which is hard to measure: vague objectives making it harder to develop a clear sense of progress;
- Accountability to many different people and organisations: all having a critical impact on the style and culture of the organisation;
- Intricate governing and management structures: built up over the years to meet particular needs and balance different interests, but often making decision-making complex and time-consuming;
- High level of volunteer input: requiring that volunteers' views are listened to and that they are actively involved in the decision-making process;
- No financial bottom line to determine priorities: profitability or discounted cashflow cannot be used to decide how resources should be allocated;
- Importance of people's values: voluntary organisations and churches have to play particular attention to people's beliefs and assumptions if they are to be effective.

All of these, but particularly the last, apply equally to management in the church. Jeavons (1992) points out that how voluntary and religious organisations achieve their objectives is just as important as what they achieve: 'the manner in which the goals are pursued can say as much about the values that the organisation wishes to promote as the goals themselves'. Treatment of staff, quality of services and where the organisation deems it ethical to raise funds send crucial messages about the organisation's values. The public expects high values in both church and non-profit organisations, and when these are not found the sense of outcry is far greater than in other sectors.

Three lessons in management

What, then, are some of the lessons from the voluntary sector for church? Three of the most critical are:

(1)   Developing a clear and agreed strategy
(2)   Building effective committee structures
(3)   Exercising positive leadership and management

Each of these are discussed below.

1.   Developing a clear and agreed strategy

Voluntary and church organisations are tempted to respond to the vast array of physical, social and spiritual need around them. This tendency, laudable in itself, makes it difficult to establish clear priorities or to say no to activities which, though deserving in their own right, simply cannot be given enough attention. As a result, time, energy and resources are watered down.

Strategic planning provides a means for dealing with some of these issues in both voluntary and religious organisations. They provide a framework which enable people to fit the practical activities of the organisation into context, as well as a broad rationale as to how resources should be allocated to different objectives and activities.

Despites its military origins ('strategy' stems from the art of directing the larger military movements of a campaign), strategic planning has been widely embraced within the sector. Concerns that strategic plans will unduly limit an organisation's flexibility and ability to respond to opportunities have not been realised. Instead they help organisations avoid overstretching themselves by providing clear and agreed priorities which, although not set in concrete, help to focus expectations, energies and resources. Similarly, while the church needs to be open to the call of God, this does not negate the value of strategic planning.

Experience of planning voluntary organisations suggests two particularly important factors in developing and implementing strategy in church organisations. The first is paying attention to the process itself. Developing strategies helps a wide range of people with different interests to see the broader picture – providing a basis for understanding and agreement. As a learning experience – reviewing the past, looking at external factors, specifying objectives – it also helps to raise particular issues in a controlled environment. As a result the design of the planning process, the involvement of different groups of people in different ways at different stages, should be carefully planned. This in turn requires the allocation of sufficient time and resources to developing the plan itself.

Secondly, the strategy needs to focus on a few issues. It is easy for plans to become very specific and detailed, with careful (and lengthy) wording obscuring rather than clarifying the central strategic decisions. The most successful plans are often those which, at a relatively early stage, have attempted to clarify the key strategic questions on which the plan needs to focus, rather than expecting it to resolve every possible issue. This in turn requires a specific review stage in which potential issues are raised in order to establish; in Argenti's words: 'What are the top half-dozen decisions that an organisation must get right in order to prosper over the next few years' (Argenti, 1989).

2.   Building effective committee structures

The development of effective forms of governance is a central topic for many voluntary organisations, particularly those with a high level of member involvement.

For many voluntary organisations committee structures have gradually evolved, adapting to accommodate specific issues and concerns as they arise. This often results in structures which are highly complex, with roles and responsibilities poorly defined and understood. The desire to ensure adequate representation and participation often conflicts with quick decision-making. Complex committee structures and systems can absorb huge amounts of energy merely to sustain them – energy which may be more usefully spent on the organisation's objectives.

Many voluntary organisations have recently spent considerable time and effort reviewing their committee structures. Three of the main trends, and their implications on church organisations, are discussed below. The first is the separation of governance and management. Committees often become involved in too much detail, duplicating the staff role. In the process, committees undermine staff and fail to see the broader picture, merely duplicating discussions which have gone on elsewhere. Spending time to clarify the respective roles of governance and management at national, diocesan and parish level is time well spent.

The second trend is the establishment of roles and objectives for each committee. For voluntary organisations this results often in a significant reduction in committees size, using other, more effective ways to consult and inform members, staff and other constituencies. In other cases it results in effective control and power being broadened out from a relatively small and unaccountable group. While some dioceses have reviewed committee structures, many feel that more could and should be done.

The third trend is the regular review of how committees work. This provides an opportunity for members to raise issues which otherwise might be difficult: cliques forming around specific issues or committee time not being spent effectively.

3.   Exercising positive leadership and management

As in the church, management is a concept which many voluntary organisations have had difficult accepting. Management can be seen very negatively – telling people what to do rather than jointly agreeing objectives and how they may be achieved, focusing on what has gone wrong rather than praising what has gone well. The practice of management can be poor, with managers attracted to the voluntary sector by a particular cause or vague desire to 'do good' rather than the wish to develop and practice managerial skills. At the same time, demands on voluntary sector managers – limited resources and unlimited needs, competing and often highly vocal interest groups, lack of clear measures of achievement – make their task especially daunting. Similar conditions apply in church organisations.

Nonetheless, voluntary organisations have increased the attention they give to management. The recruitment of experienced management from outside the sector, the development of management training and networks to support managers and successful role models has increased recognition of both the complexity and importance of good management.

Voluntary sector experience gives three pointers for church management. One is to recognise that different organisations require different types of leadership at different stages. There is no one ideal style of leadership, any more than Moses' approach to leadership would have been appropriate to Nehemiah. In making appointments to key management positions, there is a critical need to list out the key changes and characteristics which are required before making appointments.

The second is blending managerial and technical skills. Just as arts organisations need to balance artistic and managerial issues, church organisations need to achieve a suitable balance between the spiritual and the managerial. This can be done in many ways, but it invariably requires considerable time and thought.

The third is to ensure that managers – whether charity chief executives, bishops or diocesan secretaries – have clear objectives and strong support. Experience suggests that objectives are most effective when small in number (probably no more than five or six) and jointly developed by the manager and the person to whom they report. Managerial support and supervision also needs to be given considerable focus and attention. This may focus on issues such as building the senior team within the organisation, delegating decision-making and building relationships with committees and other groups. All too often training and support is focused on the lower levels within an organisation, leaving key managers under-supported and under-developed, to the detriment of the organisation as a whole.

Conclusion

While the church has much to learn from the voluntary sector, it also needs to recognise its distinctiveness. While inevitably and inextricably linked to social welfare, any analysis of the church's role would point to spirituality as its key strength. It is interesting to note in this context that many charities – especially those campaigning for change – see the battle for people's hearts and minds as central to their ethos and values. At a time when many charities and businesses are seeking to clarify and strengthen their ethos and values, the church must ensure that it does not lose its own.

Church management also needs to recognise everyone's personal accountability to God. Inevitably, people will feel pulled by God in different ways. In this context, church management needs to be seen as supporting a movement of people rather than leading a distinct organisation with clear lines of responsibility and accountability. Nonetheless, prayer and a strong sense of shared purpose help to provide cohesion and a common sense of direction.

Lastly, management in the church must be seen as serving and supporting. Christ, above all, is the supreme example of a leader leading through service, and there must be lessons for both church and secular leaders in this.

REFERENCES

John Argenti. *Practical Corporate Planning* (Unwin Paperbacks, 1989).

Mike Hudson. *Managing Without Profit: The Art Of Managing Third Sector Organisations* (Penguin, 1995).

Thomas Jeavons. 'When Management is the Message' in *Non-Profit Management And Leadership* Vol. 2 No. 4, Summer 1992.

Peter Drucker. *Managing The Non-Profit Organization* (Butterworth-Heinemann, 1990).

Charles Handy. *Understanding Voluntary Organizations* (Penguin 1990).

10

How to revive the Church

NICOLAS STACEY

I think it is now incredibly difficult to see how the Church is going to 'find the energy for renewal and turn decline into growth'. Had the Church of England made the radical changes in the 1960s that some of us were pleading for, I believe it might have been revivified. The deterioration and decline on every front in the last thirty years has been so rapid that it is operating from a much smaller base and has little room for manoeuvre. I suspect the Church that I was ordained into over forty years ago may have to collapse before it can be raised up in a new form. I see a puzzling paradox. On the one hand all the signs in our society point to us needing and yearning for the vision, the hope and the anchor that Christianity provides and yet little chance that any of the churches are going to get their message across. Such energy a fairly uninspired and unimaginative Church leadership does have is absorbed in frantic attempts to prop up a dying institution.

But if a revival is to take place it will have to come mainly through the clergy. Yet understandably, for many today their main concern is survival and who is going to pay them. With a few exceptions, mainly women, the quality (as well as the quantity) of those coming forward for ordination gives one little hope for the future. This is not surprising as in the present parochial system many of the clergy are either rushing round half a dozen or more country churches to take services for congregations in single figures, or else battling alone in a city parish or council estate serving a population of many thousands with an elderly and largely female congregation of fifty people worshipping in a decaying Victorian

119

building that seats 500! These are not inviting prospects for able young men and women who want to use their lives trying to build the Kingdom and God. Clearly an imaginative and energetic recruitment campaign to maintain the present system is a non-starter.

I believe the key to the future may be to ordain men and women as priests who are successful in key secular jobs where the real action in our society is taking place. Some may take early retirement on an adequate pension to work full time for the Church in the parochial setting but for most of them their priestly ministry will be mainly exercised in their secular work. It is critical that it is the 'successful' who are ordained. Too many of those who feel called to be non-stipendiary ministers appear to be those who haven't really 'made it' or realise perhaps subconsciously that they are not going to 'make it' in the secular world. To be ordained can be a face saver.

The ordination of a few teachers who go on to be heads of comprehensive schools, civil servants and local government officers who go on to become Chief Officers, prison staff who become Governors, wealth-creating businessmen who become managing directors, lawyers who become judges and media people of national repute would enhance the reputation of the Church and challenge people to take its message seriously. They would also provide a role model and an example to talented and ambitious young people in sharp contrast to the unflattering image of many of today's parochial clergymen. Of course I would not exclude the ordination of men and women of lesser ability working in humbler secular jobs. The non-stipendiary priest-postman, milkman and local shopkeeper can exercise an important ministry in town and village. But such is the way of the world they will provide the back-up rather than the impetus of renewal and revival.

If just for example, say, the Governor of the Bank of England was also a priest (in the way headmasters of the great public schools used to be priests), would it not say something to the thrusting and often greedy money makers in the City?

In my retirement from full time work I do a small voluntary job as assistant chaplain to the sex offender wing in a local prison. I asked one of the inmates what his fellow 'cons' and the officers thought about the Chaplain and the Church. 'Largely irrelevant' was the reply. A few years earlier when I was the Director of Social Services for the county where this prison is the Governor resigned from the prison in order to become a Methodist minister. I begged him, without success, to be ordained and stay as Governor. Had he done so, would the prisoners and officers have seen the Church as so irrelevant?

In my fourteen years as a Director of Social Services, during which one had inevitably to take many hard and painful decisions affecting the 5,000 staff in the department and the 50,000 or so people they looked after, I did not feel a contradiction or conflict with my priesthood. Should I have done?

Vibrant centres

It has been my good fortune to have been Rector of Woolwich in the 1960s heading up a team of some half dozen priests and Free Church ministers most of whom including myself combined their parochial duties with earning their living in secular occupations in the area. I have no doubt that the contribution we made to the life of the area in building the Kingdom of God was far greater than if we had all been full time parochial clergy. Two or three examples will illustrate the point. One of our priests taught RI throughout a comprehensive school of 2000 children. (In our own Sunday School, despite all our recruitment efforts, we could only muster about 50 children). Another taught Liberal Studies in a College of Further Education to young people with whom the parochial clergy would have had virtually no contact at all. Another ran a housing association for homeless families which showed the Church really caring in a practical way for all those at the bottom of the pile as well as praying for them. While I combined being Rector with being Dean of the London Borough of Greenwich and freelance journalism, with a column in the *Evening News* and *Daily Herald*. (One article in one of those newspapers earned me enough to pay a curate for a month!) The only hope that I can see for the Church in our inner-city and council estate areas is drastically to reduce the number of church buildings, many of which are an appalling drain on resources and of little architectural merit, and create a few strong, preferably multi-denominational and multi-purpose, centres manned by a team of priests, ministers and Christian laypeople, virtually all of whom would be working in key secular positions in the community by coming together for worship and prayer to give a warm and vibrant centre to the local congregation which people would feel was worth joining.

In country areas where congregations have decreased by 37% over the last twenty or so years village churches, many of which are medieval gems, cannot be closed or converted. Other remedies are required. Here the future lies with men and women from the local congregation serving as non-stipendiary priests on a part-time and largely voluntary basis. There are many outstanding lay people who have taken early retirement who are looking for an opportunity for service and who, amongst others, would be strong candidates for a massively increased non-stipendiary ministry.

Of course there will always be the need for some fulltime priests, Bishops and cathedral Deans. But just as a cabinet minister can switch from being Home Secretary to Chancellor of the Exchequer, top civil servants from one ministry to another and businessmen from running an oil company to a railway, so I believe non-stipendiary could move to being Bishops and Deans. We are living in the contract culture and a five or ten years spell for a non-stipendiary as, say, Dean of Westminster could be a creative experience for both the man or woman and the Abbey. I did it the other way round, moving from the full time ministry to being Deputy Director of Oxfam and then a Director of Social Services running an organisation rather more complex than a Diocese and of course with a much larger staff than any Diocesan Bishop has.

Having been Chaplain to a Bishop many years ago I can testify that the job demands much the same qualities as are required of the manager of any organisation, although I am

bound to say that somebody used to running a secular organisation would find a Bishop's lack of power and authority
very frustrating.

Crash course

Of course the question arises as to how non-stipendiary
priests should be trained. Could they afford the time? It is in
the nature of professions to surround themselves with a
mystique which is great exaggerated. I spent two years at a
well known theological college. I am sure that I must have
learnt something there other than that it is better to drink
vodka rather than gin before visiting as it doesn't make one's
breath smell. But I find it very difficult to recall that what I
learnt was any help to me as a priest in downtown areas.
What I learnt as a young naval officer was much more useful.
After all, however long you study, you are not going to learn
any more about what happened at the Resurrection. I have
been a priest for over forty years and I have largely forgotten
much of my theological training because it was irrelevant to
my work as a parish priest. In short, I think a fairly brief
crash course for intelligent and well-read laymen and women
could be devised which would adequately equip them for the
priestly ministry. Perhaps a well established theological
college could switch to providing short residential courses
backed up by a certain amount of studying at home.

The key to being an effective priest is the quality of your
life and your ability to relate to people.

Three prerequisites

For my plan to work there are a number of prerequisites. The
first is to provide a way out for those fulltime parochial
clergy who have become so dispirited that their ministries
have become counter-productive. Such men should be
offered early retirement on generous terms with opportunities for retraining, possibly as counsellors and professional
carers. As they would either not be replaced or be replaced
by non-stipendiary priests the church would save money.

Secondly, the Church hierarchy will have to change its
whole attitude to the non-stipendiary ministry. At the

moment they are seen as second class priests, useful for taking services on the Sunday after Christmas and Low Sunday (the Sunday after Easter). Yet the reality is that in many cases the non-stipendiary is abler than the incumbent. In one diocese I know the non-stipendiary priests in a group of parishes have not been asked about the needs of the Church in the area prior to a new incumbent being appointed although one of them has been regularly taking services there for over twenty years.

I can understand Bishops' uneasiness about non-stipendiary clergy. They don't have much control or authority over the stipendiary ones. They are going to have even less over the non-stipendiary. Now that local congregations are going to have to meet virtually all the costs of their clergy plus diocesan overheads, power has moved decisively from Bishop to parish. A Bishop may wish to appoint a fulltime priest to a parish but if the PCC (Parochial Church Council) is unable or unwilling to raise the stipend there is not much he can do about it.

Thirdly and most important of all: are able men and women in secular employment going to respond to a call to the non-stipendiary priesthood? Certainly not as a result of a paragraph in the parish magazine. I think there is some chance if the Diocesan Bishop was to call together twenty or thirty lay people, spell out his strategy for the Church and invite them to consider ordination. In most cases the idea will not have occurred to them. But if they saw a significant role for themselves as agents in a revivifed Church I believe some would respond. The secret would be to set a very high standard for acceptance and then it could become infectious. It's worth a try.

11

Get up and go!

PETER BRIERLEY

How to find the energy for renewal and turn decline into growth

Someone defined middle age as 'when your get up and go has got up and went'! Such was not true of John Haggai, the founder of the Haggai Institute for Advanced Leadership Training in Singapore. Thousands of Christian leaders have gone there to learn some of the necessary skills to enable the Good News to be shared in their country. In his book *Lead On!*[1] Dr Haggai outlines twelve principles he feels are essential for quality leadership. One of them is energy. His thesis is simple – no one who lacked energy ever did a significant work for the Lord.

How then do we get and maintain our energy? There are two human sources of energy, physical and mental, and the mental divide into two, negative and positive. Let us look at each of these.

Physical energy

To have enough energy for the work God has given us to do, we need the physical resources to do it. There are three of them – sufficient sleep, sufficient food, and sufficient exercise.

Sufficient sleep

The average person requires between seven and eight hours sleep a night, though some can cope with less on a regular basis, perhaps only five hours. Some can do a full day's work on much less sleep, or even none at all on an occasional basis. Margaret Thatcher often had only four hours sleep. The key organisers of the fleet of boats for the exodus from Dunkirk managed to go without sleep for five days in a row – a practice not to be recommended! Ambushed kidnappers keep themselves going for a night or so by drinking umpteen cups of coffee. Sleep is measured by grade, 0 to 4; so long as we get some in grade 4, the very deep sleep, our body copes.

Sufficient food

Every engine needs fuel to run on, and our bodies are no different. Ideally it is best to have a balanced diet for a physical 'feel good factor', and so that excess fat is not built up. When I was overweight in 1994 I lost 2 stone in six months and consequently gained an enormous amount of energy. Some are tempted to go the other way, and skip out meals, especially when they are busy. Refugee mothers sometimes foolishly give their own meagre food supplies to their children, forgetting that their children will have less chance of survival if they themselves die. One reason why so many British soldiers died building the Burma railway was simply inadequate food for the work to be done.

Sufficient exercise

Our bodies need to relax and not work all the time, even when the pace is hard. There are many ways available for exercise today, from the gym or golf club to the swimming baths, or just leaving the car at home and walking. Take your choice! But do choose something – busy church leaders often feel this is one thing that can be skipped. I was once in the cockpit of a Boeing 747. 'The best way to keep these engines going', said the pilot, 'is to fly them'. The best way to keep our bodies going is to exercise them!

Negative mental energy

We can make ourselves do things sometimes as a result of two powerful emotions: sheer anger (along with hatred and bitterness) or the milder varieties of frustration and annoyance; and personal fear, sometimes out of anxiety, sometimes out of past or potential failure. These are just as rife in Christian people as non-Christian.

Anger

Anger is a deep emotion, not always negative. When Jesus overturned the Temple tables was He just venting His anger? No, He was zealous for the glory of His Father. Sometimes as we see injustice, indifference or basic incompetence we have a real anger to do things better or to see things change so that suffering will lessen, hardship ease, or the message be proclaimed. Gareth Tuckwell is surely correct when he says, 'It is the anger in compassion that makes it a force for change'.[2] In *From Shame to Peace*[3] the Dutch psychologist Teo van der Weele recounts an experience in which he prays, 'Is there something God you are angry about?' and receives the answer, 'Yes, I am angry about the thousands of my people being killed in Ethiopia'. Teo then ponders if it could be that God still has pain today?

Paul's famous verse 'Be angry but sin not'[4] has often led Christian people to deny or repress their anger rather than express it. But that does not mean the anger has ceased, it can still cause an increased heart rate, extra adrenalin in the blood, faster breathing or other physical symptoms. Anger needs to be *resolved* if we are to find the energy for renewal. Here are four ways to consider doing that:

Sharing it can help. William Blake wrote[5]:

I was angry with my friend;
I told my wrath, my wrath did end.
I was angry with my foe:
I told it not, my wrath did grow.

Secondly, praying about your anger can help, letting it spill out as it were before God, and if shouting helps in that process, do that! God understands.

Thirdly, focusing on something rather than someone can help also. In my office I have one of those red spongee balls that can be squeezed and squeezed into any shape, as hard or as often as I like, and it then reverts to its usual roundness. It was given me by a research company, perhaps because they know the tensions research can generate! Others may go and dig the garden or clear out a cupboard. Anger may also relate to the time of life; one piece of research found those in their thirties are more likely to struggle with anger.[6]

Fourthly, physical exercise can be 'invaluable'[7] for releasing angry tension.

Fear

A fear of failure can drive many church leaders. Sometimes circumstances outside our control can cause us to fail. A large creditor goes bankrupt and we fear we may go bankrupt also. A team leader has another team member imposed upon him/her whose personality almost totally clashes, and the leader fears the likely consequential relationship failure. A colleague didn't understand one aspect of a new computer system not so long ago, and it completely failed for a whole month; she feared I would be cross (I wasn't on this occasion!).

Sometimes fear arises from low self-esteem, sheer loneliness, or lack of perception. It is not always rational, but is almost invariably subjective and relative. Fear can inhibit our taking strategic action; recently two children died in a fire in their house when they refused to jump from the first floor window to the neighbours waiting below. Fear can sap our energy, and can create its own downward spiral to total collapse. How do we avoid that and find the energy for renewal?

Firstly, be objective. Stand outside your situation as much as you can. If talking to a colleague, a senior person or a trusted totally uninvolved person, is likely to help, go ahead and talk!

Secondly, be realistic. Work out the answer to the question, 'If it does happen, so what?' When the last edition of the *UK Christian Handbook* got behind schedule, we said, 'What actually happens if we do publish it two weeks late?'

Thirdly, pray. We so often forget that prayer is the greatest power on earth. If God has the whole wide world in His hands, He surely holds our whole small world in them too.

Fourthly, ask yourself what you will learn as a result of this worry, anxiety or failure. It could be the most important lesson you ever had! God may want to change your life radically.

Positive mental energy

George Santayana, the Spanish-born American philosopher, once said, 'Fanaticism consists of redoubling your efforts when you have forgotten your aim'.[8] Positive energy flows when you are clear about your aim. As one of Frommer's travel guide advertisements said in 1994, 'Know where you're going before you get there'.[9] Vision is not just abstract idealism but practical reality in renewing your energy and seeking to turn decline into growth. 'Where there is no vision, the people perish', the book of Proverbs tells us.[10] It is not just the people who might perish with no vision, but nations, churches, organisations, leaders, and, yes, you and me. Vision is not an optional extra: it is crucial.

What is vision?

Vision needs to be put into its context. Sometimes this is given as four items:

(1) A statement of your purpose – why are you here? A question looking backwards.
(2) A statement of your mission – what are you doing? A question about your here-and-now *modus operandi.*
(3) A statement of vision – where are you going? What will you have become in five years time? Questions about the future.[11]
(4) An indication of your 'thrusts' or centres of energy, the main initiatives which will be required to bring the vision to fulfilment.

An alternative framework consists of five questions, sometimes called 'God's questions'[12] as He asked each of them initially. This is sometimes easier to work through either alone or with a Church Council, or a Board of Directors.

The first is, *Where are you?,*[13] when God called out to

Adam hiding in the garden. This includes the question, 'Why are you here?' but also seeks answers to the questions on 'What are your strengths?' and 'What are your weaknesses?' Answer each of these for your people, your products, your programmes.

The second is, *What is that in your hand?*,[14] asked of Moses when God was encouraging him to lead the Israelites out of Egypt. The staff Moses' held turned into a snake, ate other snakes, and then turned back into a branch again, but was now a very special resource. What is unique about your church, your people, your organisation, your processes? What inherent strengths do you have in these? It is important also to evaluate your culture, your values. The full set of these are usually special to each church or organisation or business.

The third is, *What are you doing here?*,[15] the question God asked Elijah after he had fled from Jezebel to Mount Sinai. What are the opportunities that you face? What are the problems that could put you down and out? What unique opportunities do you have? Summarise all your present activities in a short sentence. What motives does it reveal? How near are they to the two key priorities for a Christian – to make disciples (the Great Commission), and to mature disciples (the Great Commandment)?

Several prophets were asked the fourth question, *What do you see?*[16] Amos saw a plumbline and a basket of fruit, Jeremiah saw figs. All concrete, definitive items. What do you see as a consequence of your ministry in say five or ten years time? Do not answer with a generality, 'a larger congregation' or 'a bigger (or better) production process'. Be specific – 'fifty more members', 'planted three more churches', 'have started a ministry in debt counselling, or a luncheon club for older people', or 'have extended the church to give more facilities for youth', etc. What will *you* have become in say five or ten years time? What will the next generation of Christian leadership say about you? If you could choose one of the 80,000 verbs in the English language as your epitaph, what would it be?[17] He preached, she loved, she cared, he counted, he served, he founded, or, simply, she prayed? What do you see for yourself?

The fifth question in some ways is the most challenging for energy and renewal. It was asked of Ezekiel as he faced the valley of dry bones: *Can these bones live?*[18] When he answered that he didn't know, God told him to go forward and prophesy over them. Only after he had started to do so, did God begin to move the bones together, and form their sinews and muscles. When we don't know what to do, the way to go is – forward. As Winston Churchill said during the Second World War, 'Let us go forward together'. Find someone to go with if you can, but go forward trusting in faith that God will help you. William Carey, the pioneer Indian missionary, had this motto two centuries ago:

> Expect great things from God,
> Attempt great things for God.

The first expresses your faith, the second your vision. Both are unique to you. No one else ever has quite *your* faith, or *your* vision; they are two of the things you cannot delegate to anyone else. These alone are the source of the strength and energy you need for renewal if you are going to turn decline into growth.

NOTES

1. *Lead On!*, Dr John Haggai, Word Books, Waco, Texas, 1986.

2. *A Question of Healing*, The Reflections of a Doctor and a Priest, Gareth Tuckwell and David Flagg (Fount, London, 1995), p. 90.

3. *From Shame to Peace*, Rev Teo van der Weele, Monarch, Crowborough, Kent, 1995, p. 136.

4. Ephesians 4.26.

5. Quoted in op cit (Item 2), p. 88.

6. Quoted in *re:SEARCH*, the bulletin of the Christian Research Association, Aotearoa New Zealand, No. 9, June 1995, p. 2.

7. So Carlene Hacker, in the article 'Anger' in *Decision* magazine, May 1995, p. 29.

8. Quoted in *The International Thesaurus of Quotations* (Penguin, 1970), Section 333, Number 19. p. 221.

9. Advertisement in *The Bookseller*, January 1994.

10. Proverbs 29.18.

11. These questions are examined more closely in *Vision Building*, Peter Brierley (Christian Research, London, 1994).

12. Initially so called by Dr David Cormack, when Director of Management Training, MARC Europe, and taking a seminar on *Vision Building*, 1985.

13. Genesis 3.9.

14. Exodus 4.2.

15. 1 Kings 19.9.

16. Jeremiah 24.3; Amos 7.8, 8.1.

17. Op cit (Item 11) pp. 123, 124.

18. Ezekiel 37.3.

12

Churches as places of learning

CHRIS GONIN

Introduction

A friend at College in the 1950s used to say to me sometimes that all this thinking that we had to do – and this questioning – left him bewildered and puzzled. Then he would go past the Parish Church – and see a priest with his cassock on and feel 'Ah it is all right after all'.

Some want the church to be a place of stability in a world of change – I with others would argue that the church must be a place of learning as that offers a different security that ensures that it plays its part in the world of change.

As the reports on the Church Commissioners financial position have been reported it has felt a little like that to others. We turn up on Sunday and the church building is still there – the gathered congregation and perhaps it is all right after all. Then the reports come in that the lay giving is responding to the challenge – and thank goodness it is all going to be all right. At least that is what one half of the Ecclesiastical world want to believe – the church is saved – all is well in this changing world – my 1662 Holy Communion Service can be the stability I need.

In contrast to that, in a recent conversation, a senior manager at the Bedfordshire Training and Enterprise Council explained to me that all employees needed to see their career as a place where they were continually developing their skills so that they are more likely to be employable – they had to be learning people in a learning organisation.

Church members are not employees but the life of their congregation needs to relate to the world that men and women experience. My fortnightly calls as Chaplain have in recent weeks been in the context of a restructuring to adapt the TEC to present needs – after four years of its existence!

Why learning?

I am one of those who believes that the church – or any other modern organisation – cannot consider itself safe from the economically unstable world around it. The best we can hope for in terms of security is to be a learning people in a learning organisation as the way of managing in a world of change and especially as the resourcing of the church changes. Once we accept that the organisations are 'unfreezing'[1] from the stability they have enjoyed for so long there can be no certainty that 'refreezing' will ever take place for many years to come. So as Malcolm Grundy says elsewhere – 'One of the primary harmonising concepts is that of the "Learning Organisation", a place where ideas can be received and shared and where leadership flows from highly motivated and energised groups of people'. This is no stability but it is a way of life that can help us to manage our present dilemmas and above all the change that is happening despite ourselves.

We do not have to look very far to see change. Employment position – personal life[2] – developing countries will all effect us.

These changes reflect a deeper shift – a shift of ideas and the way old stabilities have weakened. As we celebrate VE day and VJ day who would have thought that 'ethnic cleansing' in Bosnia and Rwanda was still going to be on the agenda – fifty years after Bergen Belsen. The church and its gospel and its communication is still as crucial now as it has ever been. The church corporately and as individuals must continually face this challenge – and learn what these change of values mean – and how its own values can contribute.

Three essential strands of learning for the local congregation[3]

Our faith in Jesus Christ as the person who lived and suffered, died and rose again is unchanged. In the centuries immediately after his incarnation he was worshipped in people's homes – in medieval times he was worshipped in many places in Latin – then a great variety of Protestant and Catholic practices – by Dissenters as much as by Anglicans. The faith has remained but the adaptation to different centuries has continued – the 'pearl of great price'[4] has been held and handed on in different packaging with different emphasis – it has been managed in its presentation in very different ways. This is what I would call the first strand of a three core rope – the 'pearl of great price' to be understood and nurtured and presented in a way our new generation need to grasp it.

The second strand is the planning congregation. Elsewhere Malcolm Grundy refers to Charles Handy's sigmoid curve – always each fellowship of Christians must look to the future – and here the management skills can be applied not as an end in itself – but as presenting 'the pearl of great price' in an effective way.

The third strand is 'a managed ministry'. This is not using the techniques of management as a gimmick – but answering the question 'How can we help Ministers to best manage their task?' – however their fellowship sees that task – and however their fellowship see their ministers.

These three strands from a rope entwined together – each strand essential for each other. The metaphor like all metaphors breaks down because the entwining must be closer than the metaphor of a rope can suggest. Jesus metaphor of the Vine (John 15) is also much more alive but the three strands are not quite as clear!

New ways and new approaches for carrying 'the pearl of great price'

It is not the purpose of this paper to discuss methods of presenting the 'pearl of great price' – but it is the purpose is to say unequivocally – that 'the pearl of great price' and the values that it represents – and the way they are expressed in writing, prayer and worship, theology, pastoral care, community development and social action is fundamental. Christians may differ in the ways these various aspects of 'the pearl of great price' are expressed but what is not in doubt is that the values enshrined within it are much the same.

The purpose of this chapter is to declare that the church must continually earn new ways for the expression of the gospel – and that its task must be in these areas a 'learning organisation'. It is the conviction of this chapter that management skills can be used both to help the Minister present these values – and the local congregation to present these values by using management skills involved in planning and developing the life of the church.

Management is an art not a science needing adaptation to each organisation

There is a tendency of some to think that managing is a kind of panacea that can be lifted from a text book – or from the more impressive commercial world and dropped with little adaptation into church life. Rob Paton[5] has identified the *Social economy* as a field of work that has some distinctive features – and has with Christ Cornforth[6] identified differences between profit and non profit making organisations of which the church is clearly one. One of the features of non-profit organisations[7] is their own value systems[8] which have a powerful motivating effect. The church with its faith in Jesus Christ has a particular value system in the non-profit making world and has in each denomination its own culture. In this chapter I am not able to explore these differences but they do at the very least need to be noted as a part of our own learning about an appropriate style of management for the church.

The Planning Congregation as a learning organisation

It is not difficult to be prescriptive about the 'how' of this part of the learning organisation. It does seem important to most congregations if they are to plan that it is the *whole congregation* that does it – their learning will only happen if they are part of the process. So working out Mission or Vision statements will be of little help if the Minister – or the Deacons – or the Churchwardens do it – and tell the congregation what it is.

The Mission statement should reflect the values of the local congregation and how they see 'the pearl of great price' and its application at this point in the congregation's life. It will be a learning experience for them to do it, and then to work out that, if this is what is believed, these are the implications in real aims and measurable objectives at this stage of its life.

But some may ask what happens if the Minister changes – surely he will have to be consulted about the plan – and we will have to adapt accordingly? If the making of the plan is largely the work of the local congregation and the current minister – and the current minister learns in part what his ministry is from the local congregations plan – his job – and indeed his job description – will come out of that plan. Certainly the author would be very much helped by that process – and work out his ministry on this pattern of working. The new minister should find that in the light of the congregation plan his job is analysed – his job and person description is written and with some negotiation he has a manageable job – especially when he has more than one congregation to work with.

But again it may be protested does not the Holy Spirit come into all this – should not the local congregation 'wait' on the Holy Spirit. The other strand of 'the pearl of great price' assumes prayer worship and theology – and the planning congregation will be praying and assuming that within their planning God is at work as the writer to the Ephesians (1.4) would see it.

The Managed Minister – as essential part of the learning organisation

The minister has been managed into his vocation well in the last fifty years. Different denominations have had a thorough process of encouraging vocations, selecting candidates for training, training them at College and getting them into their first congregations. In the Anglican world the first three years or so in post has been done thoroughly with various post ordination training schemes. The author's familiarity with the post ordination experience of other priests and Ministers is very slender so there can be little comment on that.

The author in his present post felt he was lead through a variety of courses which at the beginning of his ministry here were well done by the Continuing Ministerial Education department of St Albans Diocese under the leadership of Canon Les Oglesby. It is worrying that the present financial climate seems to be threatening that process. Coupled with a Diocesan self appraisal scheme, there is much on offer which ensures a good deal of support.

This chapter argues for the development of a much more managed ministry – especially when ministers go to a new post. Again the author has attended a new posts conference – and subsequently tutored on one – and felt it was a good and useful course for himself and others. With the freehold under review, for example for Anglicans, is it not time to think in terms of a supervision and appraisal scheme that is not only more direct but also compulsory? The minister is a very expensive resource – and a crucial one, surely the time has come when the laity should expect that their minister is answerable and accountable directly for his ministry.

This process could start with a job analysis which leads to a job description and person description prepared by the congregation in co-operation with the Supervising Minister or Bishop for that congregation at that time – clearly differing as the congregation moves on to a different stage in its development. Advertisement, competitive interview, and appointment on the basis of the job and person description with clear tasks worked out by the congregation for the next few years. Much of the training experienced by newcomers to the St Albans diocese would be appropriate but particular training for the particular parish with particular supervision for that setting would strengthen the effectiveness of the Minister. Space does not allow for the details of that to be set out – but there is room for experienced clergy working in a similar setting to supervise on behalf of the Bishop or

Supervising Minister. In the light of recent events at Lincoln a more appropriate grievance and disciplinary scheme would be appropriate.

Conclusion

The metaphor of a rope with its three strands suggest a way in which a local congregation could become a learning organisation to manage the changes of our times. Each strand is essential for the whole – and yet to focus on each strand and their interrelationship with the others could produce a creative learning congregation in relation to its environment. 'The pearl of great price' – one biblical symbol for the Kingdom demands the creation of 'congregations' that require the stimulus of the two disciplines of theology and management that not only stimulates learning but also effectiveness.

REFERENCES

1. Open University course B789 'Managing Voluntary and Non-profit making organisations'.

2. *Something to celebrate* – Church House Publishing 1995.

3. For the sake of this paper the aspect of the Church considered will be the local worshipping community – and the word 'congregation' will be used to include the Anglican concept of the parish, the Baptist concept of the local fellowship, the Roman Catholic concept of the parish and the free church concept of the 'gathered community'.

4. St James Authorised Version – Matthew 13.46.

5. Bob Paton The Social economy: Value-based Organisations in the Wider Society in '*Issues in Voluntary and Non-profit management*' edited by Julian Batsleer, Chris Cornforth and Rob Paton (1991 – Addison Wesley).

6. Bob Paton and Chris Cornforth: 'What's different about Managing in Voluntary and Non-profit Organisations', in *Issues in Voluntary and Non-profit management* edited by Julian Batsleer, Chris Cornforth and Rob Paton (1991 – Addison Wesley).

7. The Open University course B789 'Management in Voluntary and Non Profit Enterprises'.

8. *Managing Volunteers* – The Volunteer Centre UK – 1992).

13

Quality ministry

JOHN WALKER

The application of quality standards (BS5750, ISO9000)
to the Church Ministry

What is 'quality' when applied to church ministry? A group of clergy and lay people in Southwell Diocese began asking that question in 1993. Management Consultants, RIVA in West Yorkshire, generously gave us free advice and their time to explore the concept, because they too were interested in the answer to the question, as applied to the Church.

After two years research and application of the quality standard, we not only had an answer, but have also formed a group to 'promote the principles and good practice of Quality in Ministry in Southwell Diocese'.[1]

Quality ministry is about the church's service to its members and to the community. It is about meeting our own and our 'customers' expectations of what the church offers. 'By their fruits you shall know them' – by the way we deal with and process baptism enquiries, wedding preparation, PCC meetings, nurture programmes, the care of church-yards, the integration of new members into the church, and much more, we are being judged by the quality of what we are doing and how we are doing it.

Quality service is also about collaborative ministry. It calls for and necessitates the minister and people to be involved from the outset in brainstorming best practice. So for

---

1. The first Aim of QIM in the constitution. Inaugural AGM was 27th April 1995.

example as you will read later, Haydon Wilcox, the vicar of three rural parishes in Nottinghamshire worked with his already established baptism team to produce a consistent and effective ministry to those parents seeking baptism for their children in his parishes.

Quality involves 'writing it down'. BS5750 and ISO9000 quality standards in industry are documented management systems (DMS). As Val Rampton describes in her story about Leaving a Parish, she welcomed the insights of a Documented Management System when she moved from one parish to another.

Writing down the ideas from the brainstorming session at the beginning and then setting out the detailed work instructions have proved to be an invaluable tool in empowering and training lay people in our churches. This documenting and the crucially important business of updating documents has also proved to be a very effective means of evaluating the ministry and work of the church.

Documented Management System

The total quality approach in the manufacturing and service industries depends on a documented management system. This is the approach we have applied to ministry. There are three documents involved: *The Quality Manual* – which is the policy statement, *The Procedure* – which describes the steps in the process, and finally the *Work Instruction Document* which is the largest document and details all the instructions for each step of the Procedure.

The following two stories illustrate the working of a quality ministry approach.

1.   A PARISH STORY by Haydon Wilcox

Our story at St Margaret's, Bilsthorpe, started without our Baptism Team being involved with the formation of a documented management system for the Baptism of Infants. We were fortunate that we had done some essential groundwork; there was a Church Council policy and there was a trained team whose responsibilities went from initial contact with an enquiring parent to the aftercare of the child and their family five years from the actual baptism or service of thanksgiving for the birth of a baby.

The purpose in creating the documented management system was initially a personal project but it soon became owned by the Baptism Team as an invaluable tool for consistency and effectiveness.

Once we had identified the scope of our work and defined each step needed we were surprised and affirmed by realising what a lot was involved. As we formulated, scrutinised and developed our working instructions we could understand the roles of each person and the way their responsibilities dovetailed together. Defining each part of the process in fact built up the team, especially as we all began to improve and refine the system. Often people who were not directly involved in one part of the baptism procedure helped others who were to improve their function so that, eventually, it could benefit everyone.

As an outcome, the documented management system has helped us to know more clearly what we are individually doing and enables each member to grasp a vision of the whole. As all were involved it meant that this document was owned by the team. Without a policy or some working experience I don't think we would have gained as much as we did from the process. Having the documented management system means that training a new member of the team will be much simpler and can in fact be done by a number of people. It is also a document that allows us to review the whole process – something which has already taken place. It also helps others in the Church to know what actually is involved in this ministry and again this is an affirming and self-regulating process within the whole parish church.

We feel sure we are offering quality ministry to parents who seek baptism for their child and that all enquirers are treated with equality. They gain an impression of ministry being focused within a team of caring and sensitive Christians and not just the Vicar.

2. LEAVING A PARISH by Val Rampton

The first four meetings of the DMS group coincided with my leaving one parish (where I was in charge of a daughter

church in a large parish) and moving to another situation –
to take charge of a group of three rural parishes. Just after
this another member of the original DMS group also moved
parishes so we were able to exchange experiences.

The whole process of leaving raised a lot of questions:
who needs telling about the move? Who takes over the
care of particularly delicate pastoral situations? How will
different areas of responsibility be covered until someone
new is appointed? Which groups and individuals will need
a 'last visit'? How can the leaving be made a positive
one? In summary, how does one 'leave well'? I looked in
vain for anything written down about this – but there is
nothing.

Later, I contrasted my arrival at the daughter church five
years previously with my arrival in the new parishes. When I
arrived at the daughter church my predecessor had left well
ordered papers. Folders had been left covering all aspects of
the church life; 'Youth work' with subsections for different
ages: 'Church building' with subsections on gas, health, fire,
insurance, etc: and many other folders. Anything of value
from the man previous to him had been included, but the
paper had been carefully 'pruned' – nothing unnecessary was
included. There were also notes about the church neighbour-
hood, lists of key people, accounts of how various areas of
church life happened, and so on. It was invaluable in getting
to grips with the new work.

When I had been in the new parishes for a short while,
each church presented me with several cardboard boxes from
the previous incumbent – there were also several boxes in the
wardrobe at the Vicarage. The boxes were an absolute
shambles. Historical records that should have been in the
Diocesan Archives Officer were mixed with papers that
could be thrown in the bin; reports of old school governor
meetings were mixed with old candles from Christmas
services. Recent records were muddled up with those from
incumbent back from the 1950's. There were also mildewed
copies of Compline, a choir hat, a cloth money bag, puri-
ficator, several collecting boxes, even the thurible from one
of the churches. Some items which church members had
wanted for some time came to light, but essential informa-

tion on some matters was missing, and still has not come to light nine months on.

This experience sharpened up the earlier questions about 'Leaving well'. If one person leaves well, then that is an enormous help to the church, and to the new person coming in. If someone leaves 'badly', then he/she may be saved a lot of trouble, but a great deal of trouble is left for others.

The DMS group took this on board and produced procedure and working instructions for 'leaving a parish'. We felt that it would be an enormous help to incumbents and parishes if such a document was widely available. We are sure that such documents would be welcomed by many. Not only the document themselves, but also the way in which they had been drawn up and regularly updated, facilitating the work and mission of the church.

CONCLUSION

From these stories we can conclude that the benefits of a quality ministry are as follows.

For the individual church member it promotes growth and holiness, a greater confidence and ownership of parish ministry. It also facilitates a deeper sense of belonging and even helps to identify leaders in the church. For the congregation it is a tool for collaborative ministry – a much talked about subject but rarely are we advised exactly how this collaboration is supposed to work! For the deanery, district or diocese, our brief experience suggests that this can be a means of sharing best practice, and of fostering unity and consistency in some of the areas we work in.

The downside of all this is that it would seem to involve more paperwork for the clergy and more bureaucracy. There is the fear too that 'business techniques are not suitable for the church'. We could argue that the church has had a DMS from its earliest days! The Old Testament scriptures were our first documents and were soon added to. Our Quality in Ministry group believes we are doing nothing more radical than adding some modern disciplines to our ancient traditions.

Another fear about a DMS ministry is that it 'threatens the

clergy' – i.e. it takes power away from them and exposes ineffectiveness and lack of expertise. Virtually anything which emphasises collaborative ministry threatens the clergy and that is something which we have to recognise and be realistic about. DMS promotes *real power* which is about people following their leader and having a sense of ownership and involvement with the work of the church.

A quality approach to ministry *will* expose weaknesses but it also helps with identifying training needs in both minister and congregation. Indeed it has also helped with motivating people to seek training.

A word of warning

Finally, a church using a Documented Management System should not let its procedures which have been painstakingly drawn up be cast into stone. We should be seeing continual improvement in the quality of our ministry through regular review, thus creating all the necessary room for spontaneity, new insight, creative thinking; all of which adds up to a proper dependency on the Spirit of God informing and influencing the work of the gospel.

14

Quality at work

MALCOLM PEEL

The 1986 International Standards Organisation (ISO) vocabulary defines 'quality' as:

> The totality of features and characteristics of a product or service that bear on its ability to satisfy stated or implied needs.

This definition implies knowledge of the requirements of the customer, thus placing him or her at the centre of the concept of quality. It also suggests that quality applies not only to faults of manufacture (e.g. something that breaks in use) but also to poor design (i.e. something that does not do what the customer requires).

The definition covers both products or services, but quality assurance has historically been applied far more frequently within manufacturing industry than in other sectors. It is, after all, easier to assess the quality of a widget than of a doctor's consultation.

Industry and commerce have, in recent years, become deeply quality-conscious, and there has been an increasing realisation of the harmful effects of lapses in quality. These include:

(a) the costs of scrap and time lost on the production and correction of defective products,
(b) the costs of handling complaints,
(c) compensation payments,
(d) litigation, with its legal costs and possible payment of direct and indirect damages,

(e) criminal actions for infringement of Health and Safety and similar legislation,

(f) overall customer dissatisfaction and more or less serious loss of market.

This growing concern about quality has, over the past three decades, worked through the various sectors of the UK economy. Attitudes first changed in some sectors of manufacturing industry, especially those producing consumer goods (e.g. motor manufacturers), often under pressure from the growing competition from Japan. Some service areas (such as air transport) followed fairly rapidly; application in others has lagged. Extension to the public sector (including health, education, local and central government activities) has been partly achieved by devices such as Citizens' Charters, although their effectiveness may be open to question. Some professional areas (such as the law, accountancy, surveyors, etc) may still be felt to require action.

A number of approaches to quality assurance have been used. These include:

(a) inspection and test
(b) quality circles
(c) 'right first time'
(d) total quality management
(e) customer service
(f) accreditation

We will now look briefly at each of these in turn.

Inspection and Test

The traditional approach to ensuring quality in the product has been to inspect or test it during or after manufacture.

Inspection may be carried out at a number of stages during manufacture, to check whether individual parts or assembles meet the required standard. It is almost always carried out to some extent on the finished product. If the product has critical safety implications – parts of aero-engines, or brake systems on cars for example – thorough inspection is essential. In other situations, inspection of a sample is regarded as sufficient. Working out how many or how frequently to sample and interpreting the results calls for quite complicated statistical planning and analysis.

Some producers, including some car manufacturers during the 1960s, were slow to recognise the shift from a suppliers' to a buyers' market, and carried on leaving the customer to complain of faults. The loss of customer goodwill was felt at that time to be less important than the financial savings.

Inspection has a number of drawbacks. The most serious of these is the cost; the more complete the process, the more costly. It must always cause delay, which can be severe. The separation between production personnel and inspectors may cause tensions, and will certainly lessen the degree of responsibility felt by the producers. Thorough inspection may not always be easy to carry out; despite modern techniques such as X-ray and ultrasonic testing, some faults are almost impossible to detect.

Inspection will, in some form and to some extent, always remain a necessary part of manufacturing process. However, its effects are mostly negative. If carried out efficiently, it should prevent the great majority of defective products from reaching customers although no system can completely eliminate these. But inspection can only contribute to quality improvement by alerting those involved to the kind and frequency of faults.

Testing is invariably carried out during the design and development of new products to make sure that they work properly and reliably (or indeed that they work at all!). This may be done in a laboratory or on a test-bed, in some special environment, such as a test track for cars, or perhaps by customers under more or less controlled conditions. It will be necessary to produce, as far as possible, the range of situations under which the product is expected to be used. Thus, for example, a photographic film must take pictures and withstand storage both in the tropics and the arctic winter. Manufacturers may decide that a product must be tested 'to destruction' – that is, until the weakest aspect of its fails.

A very small number of services (such as classroom teaching) are subject to inspection; the great majority are not. Inspection of many others (e.g. rail travel, nursing care, etc) has been seen as difficult to carry out systematically, intrusive to customers or damaging to employee morale. Customer surveys have been used to provide information in these areas, but may not produce much sound, objective data. Testing of new services is also rare; they are often set up without any piloting or prior testing.

Quality Circles

Concern about the success of Japanese competition during the 1970s and 1980s led to careful examination of their approach to quality, followed by adoption in the West of several of their concepts. One of the first was the approach known as 'Quality Circles'. Quality Circles are regular meetings of those involved in a particular operation – usually but not always shop-floor manufacturing – to discuss quality issues and agree improvements. The members of the Circle will include those carrying out the various processes, supervisors, managers, and possibly members of other departments involved in the operation.

The direct aim of Quality Circles is to identify recurring problems and to propose solutions. In most case, they will have authority to implement changes. Their great indirect advantage is the feeling of ownership of quality problems and their solutions. Problems are less likely to be seen as the responsibility of another department, of 'management', or of no one in particular. Any changes needed are more likely to be implemented whole-heartedly.

Effective Quality Circles can produce immediate improvements in quality, but are not always suitable or effective unless combined with other approaches. Quality Circles are much rarer in service-type operations, but there is no reason why they could not be equally effective in this environment.

'Right First Time'

This approach to quality improvement aims at creating a climate in which all employees become quality conscious. It may involve analysis and removal of the causes of quality lapses, and employee training. It may be associated with other approaches, especially Total Quality Management.

Total Quality Management (TQM)

The concept of Total Quality Management was developed and widely applied during the 1980s. It is based on the twin beliefs that satisfaction of customer requirements is central to the work of every organisation, and that every individual in an organisation has a crucial role in providing that satisfaction. The roles of 'supplier' and 'customer' are extended to embrace all internal relationships. Thus even those who have no direct responsibility with the final customer understand that their every action will affect the final results.

Implementation of TQM requires acceptance of the basic philosophy throughout the organisation. For success, the highest levels must be committed and seen to be committed. It is usual to establish a task group to provide continuing motivation and drive the process forward. The help of external consultants specialising in this approach is often used.

The steps in the TQM process will usually include: definition of the organisation's vision, often defined in a 'Mission Statement'; establishing the expectations of customers, suppliers and employees; reviewing current standards of performance and the reasons for failures; producing a strategy for improvement; implementing the strategy (invariably including training); and monitoring subsequent performance.

TQM is often felt to have produced improvements in final quality and in the internal processes needed to ensure that quality. It has, however, been interpreted in a variety of ways, and has been a particularly fruitful field for consultants of varying degrees of effectiveness. Its main benefits spring from the insistence, at every level, on the central place of customers and their needs.

Customer Service

Since the mid 1980s, there has been increasing focus on the customer as the main reason for any organisation's existence, and the only reach touchstone of quality. The main drive of organisations varies: some are driven by profits; some, especially in the public sector, by a kind of inertia or even the desire to provide employment for their staff; many are driven by pride in their products. But the customer service philosophy emphasises that the main drive must be the customer. Moreover, in every sector, the way it is delivered is at least as important as the product (or service). The finest dish will fail to please if it is banged down on the table by a surly and ill-mannered waiter. The most desirable car will make its new owner unhappy if it supplied after a long and unexplained wait, with a number of minor faults, in the wrong colour, by an unhelpful salesman who mixes up the paperwork with that of another customer.

This approach begins from a systematic attempt to establish what the needs of the customer are, followed by action to meet those needs. Surveys may help, especially in large markets, but the key is real closeness and readiness to listen to the customer by every member of an organisation. The process must be continual; customer needs and organisational performance change over time. Customers, for example, who twenty years ago were prepared to accept a six month wait for a telephone connection, a standard black handset, and perhaps a share of a 'party line' now expect connection within days, an infinite range of telephone styles, colours and functions, and the ability to connect with the network in ways which suit their individual needs.

This approach to quality is one of the few that has been applied most frequently to the service sector. It began in the retail area, and was extended to some organisations in passenger transport, banking and a small number of public services and professions. It has a long way still to go, despite its political endorsement in the form of various citizens' or customers' 'Charters'.

Accreditation

Increasingly, accreditation by an external body against established standards has been used as a motor to bring about quality improvements. Within the UK, the British Standard BS 5750 was extensively used. This has now been incorporated into the virtually identical group of International Standards Organisation's ISO 9000–9004 standards. These standards are not, as is sometimes thought, quality standards for the finished product or service; it remains entirely for the producing organisation to set their own standards. The standards are for the *quality systems* used, but here also they are not prescriptive; an organisation may establish its own systems within a basic framework of good practice. Accreditation against the standard indicates that the chosen quality systems are being correctly and consistently followed.

The concept of accreditation originated in manufacturing industry, and its application to service sectors has followed more slowly. The wording of the standard remains easier to apply to goods than services. Like other initiatives, the process of obtaining accreditation must start from the highest level, and involves: appointment of a quality manager, choice of a registration body with scope for the organisation, obtaining the commitment of all staff, drawing up a quality plan, setting up and documenting procedures, auditing the application of the procedures, and being assessed. Accreditation must be renewed at regular intervals.

There is a degree of debate between those who see accreditation as a helpful discipline and those who fear it as a largely bureaucratic process imposing additional work, costs and rigidity. Accreditation of suppliers against ISO 9000 is now frequently demanded within the public sector, and there is no doubt that this has given impetus to an approach which might otherwise not have gained such widespread acceptance. The 'Kitemark' offered is also seen as a marketing advantage, even though its significance may not always be fully understood.

The Bottom Line

As with so many things, there is not, and never will be, a magic solution to the problems of quality assurance. Each of the approaches described has been found helpful when efficiently adopted in appropriate circumstances. None can be sufficient on its own, and none will continue to be effective for ever. The very act of introducing a new approach once in a while will, like the new broom, sweep cleaner, but only for a while.

The essential ingredients of quality must, however, remain the same: thorough understanding of the customer's needs; commitment to their satisfaction by everyone; and a refusal ever to rest on our laurels.

15

Appropriate professional support and development

HILARY INESON *and* BERNARD KILROY

'WHAT ARE THE MOST APPROPRIATE WAYS OF FOSTERING THESE FOR THE ORDAINED?'

Many readers will open this chapter with the apprehension we had: how could we possibly reflect all the subtleties needed as well as the circumstances of different denominations? We wanted to be sure of not being unduly influenced by the forms which happen to be available now and yet to build on existing provision wherever possible.

Our agenda included in particular: understanding self and personal development; interpersonal skills; understanding process; leadership where lay people are increasingly taking up roles previously held by the ordained; understanding organisations, whether groups, bureaucracies, federations or networks; managing with volunteers; working with the other gender. Yet we realised this list was influenced by current concerns. Hence the first part of our chapter tries to put together a definition which is complete yet flexible; our second part explores its implications.

Defining The Issue

The spontaneous demand by clergy themselves for professional development is not widespread and expresses itself in very different ways. One of our major purposes was also to try to articulate what latent and future demand there might be. Then there are central pressures to set up systems of development with varying objectives. These can be received with enthusiasm but sometimes have been under-used or resented.

Unfortunately, any calls for rationalistation may be interpreted as demands for greater control. The balance is struck by David Shepherd, the Anglican Bishop of Liverpool, a diocese where a ministry review process is well established. In the introduction to a recent book on ministry development and appraisal, he emphasises 'there can be few more pressing needs in the church of today than the provision of adequate and appropriate support for those called to the ordination ministry'.[1] Indeed, it is acknowledged informally that one impetus towards ministerial review has been to avoid clergy breakdown.

In Roman Catholic dioceses, where episcopal control has usually been strong, formal systems of ministry appraisal are rare, yet schemes of personal development by dioceses since the 1970s, when numbers leaving the priesthood were especially high, have achieved participation rates of around two thirds of all priests.[2]

Both the Methodist[3] and United Reformed[4] churches emphasise the supportive dimension in their new plans for clergy self appraisal, facilitated on the one hand by an 'accompanist' and on the other by a 'companion', with the main aim to identify development needs, whether personal or professional. In similar vein, the Baptist fostering of professional development via sabbaticals and grants towards further study couches its language in terms of encouragement[5] and there are echoes of this with the Black majority churches.

Main 'longitudinal' axis

In order to articulate our definition, we have tried to portray the main themes as a diagram (Figure 1). If ministry in its professional context is the main longitudinal axis, at one pole is the emphasis on the personal calling, often understood as enabling the minister to act as mediator of the divine and for which *spiritual direction* or *counselling* may be the

MINISTRY AS PERSONAL CALLING

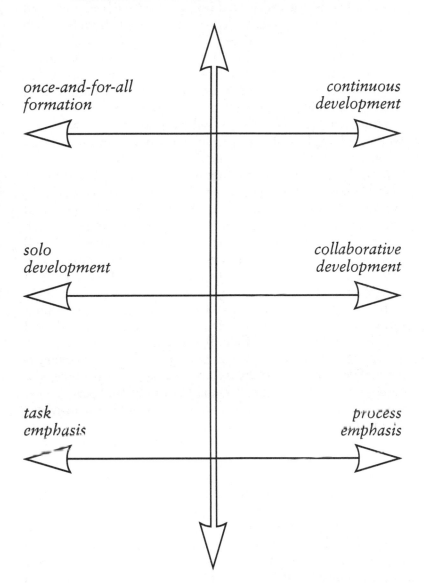

MINISTER AS ORGANISER OF CONGREGATIONS

Figure 1   Polarities of Professional Ministry

most appropriate form of 'professional' development (if professional is not considered inappropriate here). The need can be most acute when clergy are seen as models which people then love to destroy.

This axis passes very tangibly into the professional mode as it moves towards the other pole – the pastor in his or her organisational role, whether as animator of worship or as coordinator of a congregational unit. Here, professional development is likely to be formally assisted by *work consultancy*, perhaps linked in some way to *appraisal* or *ministerial review*.

It is all too easy to see these poles as 'either/or' alternatives This is a particular danger where the individual spiritual calling, endowed by sacrament, is emphasised exclusively and underscored by writings on ministry development which ignore the more mundane terminology of 'overseer' and 'administrator' used by the early church. The organisational dimension may then be seen as a necessary evil; such tension is a traditional theme.

The tension may be masked unconsciously by grouping professional relationships within the terms of 'pastoral' and 'mission', which are sufficiently broad to be open to any interpretation, including being entirely spiritual and evangelistic. The tension may be reinforced by circumstance; the country parson or inner city chaplain may well feel cut off from the distant organisation which is preaching teamwork; morale and motivation are often dependent on participation.

Or, because ministerial review systems are something thought of as part of planning for promotion, ministers may not discuss their concerns openly. Canon Ian Hardaker, clergy appointments advisor in the Church of England wrote in 1990: 'I am concerned by the number of men and women whom I see and with whom I discuss their present work and their style of ministry who express an appreciation of the questions I ask and the interest I show. Many say that this is the first time anyone has ever shown that degree of interest in them and their work'.[6] This does suggest that many clergy are looking for care given in a structured and regular manner.

The axis in our diagram is intended as a continuum which clergy move up and down all the time, as happens with part-

nership, leadership, parenthood, marriage, friendship. These
are activities *and* relationships, sometimes by turns, sometimes at the same time. Indeed, the mark of an effective
minister, as of any effective manager, or partner, leader,
parent, spouse or friend is the ability to adapt appropriately
to the requirements of the situation.

There are parallels within the professions generally, particularly in the sea change in management awareness during the
last half century. Most professions originally established
themselves as individual specialists, performing within
defined standards and ethical conduct. In such a context,
management was minimalist, concerned with records,
contracts of employment, office management and ledgers. In
professional training, 'administration' was a minor adjunct
and did not figure in any continuing education; you learnt on
the job.

The world in which professionals act has changed in three
main ways, driving them to recognise a managerial dimension. This applies in a variety of fields, such as medicine,
education, engineering, law, accountancy, and architecture.
First, professionals are working increasingly as *organisations*
and so can be preoccupied with alternative forms of working
together in teams and every member partnerships which seek
to avoid the hierarchies and bureaucracy, which too many
still see as synonymous with organisation.

Secondly, the work environment of management has
become far more *complex*, requiring choices, to envision the
future, to make strategy, to plan, to programme, to organise,
to evaluate and to communicate. Thirdly, management focus
has shifted from maintenance of existing situations towards
management of *change*, requiring as much attention on
process as on task, new conceptions of leadership, interactive
skills, and a recognition of the 'learning organisation'. Of
course, such trends can be resisted, for instance by preserving
past patterns of organisation, management and interaction –
but only at the risk of endangering the health of the institutions, their purpose, and their morale.

All voluntary organisations from Oxfam to parent-teacher
associations have an additional level of complexity in the
subtlety of the psychological contract; workers feel the

organisation is *theirs*. Churches have further complications because they play such diverse roles within their local communities. Within the churches, that diversity is compounded because the boundaries of ministry and mission are unclear and because the concept of ministry itself is changing. Therefore, the definition of management within ministry, and thus of its professional support and development, must accommodate all these convoluted dynamics.

Three 'lateral' axes

Across the main longitudinal axis, Figure 1 portrays three minor and lateral axes. The first towards the 'personal' end is the polarity between 'once and for all' ministerial formation prior to ordination and the growing emphasis in all the main denominations on continuous development. The rationale can be traced very explicitly in documents of the Anglican church since 1980[7] and of the Roman Catholic church since 1990,[8] recalling earlier canon law.

Parallels can be found with the modern development of 'lifelong learning' in management education; indeed professional bodies are frequently now requiring continuous renewal of qualifications as a condition for retaining chartered status. However, in ministry, continuous development seems to have as much to do with the very old tradition of the lifelong spiritual pilgrimage. In the documents quoted, this emphasis remains in the Roman Catholic, whereas the Anglican does have a stronger managerial and organisational dimension to its pastoral considerations. Also in practice, in all the main denominations, energy and finance are still concentrated overwhelmingly on ministerial formation, which tapers off during the first three to five post ordination years, sometimes formally termed 'probation'.

A second and middle lateral axis we have portrayed as a polarity between solo development and collaborative development. Once again, one might draw parallels with the emphasis on synergy and teamwork in modern management education. However, this fruitful tension has existed in the church since the earliest times, not just between the lone prophet and the shared agape feast, but also even within monasticism itself, between the hermit and the community.

Collaboration is an ambiguous term meaning either between ordained ministers or between clergy and laity. The background report to the 1980 Anglican synod resolution suggested '... there will be some occasions when clergy and laity may most appropriately learn together and from each other'. However, our perception is that such activities, whether as sabbaticals, conferences or courses, still frequently remain separated, though linked, in spite of the avowals about 'every member ministry' and the 'universal priesthood of all believers'.

A third and organisational lateral axis we have portrayed as a polarity between the task emphasis on efficient and structured procedures on the one hand and on the other the 'sentient', organic and process dimension of the organisation, its cultures and styles and values, in other words what makes it gel and tick.

It would be useful to research the extent to which clergy identify development needs as mainly in the task area or the process area. Even so, a process issue can be wrongly identified as a task or procedural issue merely because it then becomes more tangibly 'manageable'. Also, the somewhat mechanistic assumptions of classical management have become conventional wisdom in the West since the 1920s. Thus, for instance, selection procedures or organisational structures can be over formalised on the assumption that this is more 'professional' or 'business-like'.

Such preoccupations can distract attention from the key importance of the psychological contract and the 'learning organisation'. These are the means by which an organisation recognises and responds to the changing needs and views of its members, its customers, its clients, its 'stakeholders' (i.e. all those having an interest in its activities). In the future, the ordained could play a key role as educators and facilitators in such a learning organisation. However, they will frustrate development if their primary concern is with being a 'good administrator'.

'Positioning' within the system

The diagram may help to 'plot' current preoccupations of individuals or of groups or indeed of institutions. Then, one might ask: 'If that's where I/we/they are, is that where I/we/they want to be?' The next stage is to consider the implications and options open to those who are seeking to use or to provide professional development in the light of this.

To illustrate, traditionally the tendency has been to concentrate on the 'personal calling/once-and-for-all/solo' quadrant. It is becoming increasingly necessary to move towards the organisational end of the main axis, perhaps because of greater numbers or groups to coordinate or in order to establish some kind of contract with paid or voluntary helpers. The natural inclination may be to gravitate towards a mechanistic kind of organisation and to assume that there is no alternative style, unless by softening it through a 'human relations' approach, which can then be seen as manipulative.

In other words, the diagram has been drawn on the assumption that there is a natural tendency for a traditional longitudinal axis towards the left hand side of the diagram. If it is felt necessary to move the whole axis to the right, then the new continuum needs to be consistent.

If, for instance, there is a greater propensity to move laterally towards lifelong learning than to move towards collaborative patterns and at the same time there is a tendency to work in the organisational area in a formally structured way, then the main axis can become unnaturally angled. Lifelong learning these days invariably means the willingness to incorporate a new and interactive approach.

Alternatively, when two parties are involved, say, when a pastor whose axis lies naturally down the open 'right hand' side of the diagram encounters for the first time a congregation whose expectations lie along the traditional 'left hand' side, there will be difficulties of understanding and therefore difficulties of adjusting to one another. Other scenarios might be between a bishop and incumbent or a minister and the stewards in a congregation. The means of professional support must be able to accommodate both dialogue and growth.

When we analysed all these factors, we realised that the system needed for professional support and development in ministry needs to take into account the different emphases of ministry, and to be recognised as authentic, as well as to adapt to changing circumstances. The definition emerged as a sequence portrayed as a cyclical diagram (Figure 2) and expressed as follows:

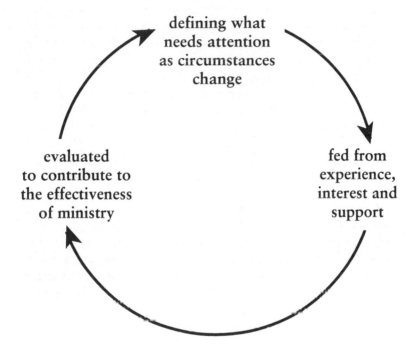

Figure 2   System of professional support modelled

We need a system of professional development for ministry in its widest sense which will draw out what needs attention as circumstances change. It must use a range of resources and methods, fed from the experience, interest and support of the whole church, both lay and ordained. It must be monitored and evaluated in order to contribute to the effectiveness of ministry and its shape in a changing world and changing church context.

What could that mean in practical terms, and how different would that be from existing patterns, hence the second part of this chapter?

Practical Implications of the Definition

Defining what needs attention as circumstances change ...

The scope of attention for professional development could be generally widened beyond what is common now, beyond a narrow emphasis on administrative functions yet not going to the other extreme of a preoccupation with personal development programmes. The definition of ministry might embrace ministry teams, which would (perhaps with other teams) explore their development together, since the learning experience tends to be anchored with the group in which it first takes place. Hence, where that learning is collaborative between the ordained and non-ordained, many of the facilitators should be lay in order to ensure an open agenda.

The fulcrum of the learning process could be a managerial theology such as that developed by Peter Rudge,[9] and would need to be related to other models of church, revelation, power and community. This theology might be deepened with reference to the crucial tension between nature and grace. The activities and tasks of ministry – typically to do with the managing of *people*; with other *resources* especially finance; and with *buildings and plant* – would then be derived from this modelling and be integral to ministry rather than stand in their own right, as if add-ons to faith. Otherwise, secular and alien patterns are in danger of being imposed.

Attention would be upon purposes rather than upon means. Instead of speaking about the managing *of* people, a theme of 'service' would be about managing *with* people for ministry purposes. This would have less of a personnel preoccupation which contains strong elements of the formal contract for paid workers. It would be a cluster of concerns with a more flexible boundary, including voluntary relationships and behavioural and inter-personal matters. Instead of managing resources, especially finance, through attention to techniques and procedures, a theme of *'stewardship'* would integrate as well as interrogate the purposes and processes of resources for ministry, including goodwill. Instead of a preoccupation with managing buildings and plant, a theme of the *'presence'* of ministry would include the whole dimension of communication, media and witness within the 'transaction' for faith, focusing on the benefits generated by the 'offering'.

Once the organisational dimension of ministry is understood in a more open way, methods of learning are likely to be more exploratory, more oriented towards discernment and reflection, more based on the juxtaposition of ministers' experience with their faith and scripture. Consequently, the method of study and exchange of ideas is likely to be less through set courses of study, previously favoured by theological colleges and seminaries, and more towards the work consultation methods practised through animators and facilitators by agencies such as the previous Avec.[10]

Distance learning has already begun through some theological colleges. Correspondence material is made real through periodic seminars and eventually might become more interactive through computerised programmes. At present, methods are at an elementary stage compared with, say, what is offered by the Open College or the Open University. Although development will be inhibited by the expense of investment costs, they also will make possible the 'devolution' of the learning process to local centres and encourage networking between them.

Fed from experience, interest and support ...

A new dynamic will be created as the focus of learning is shifted towards reflection on actual experience rather than on theoretical principles and the more broadly the dimension of ministry is understood. The centre of gravity then shifts from a corpus of knowledge *at* a theological college towards the process of ministry within the actual parish or the congregation facilitated by staff *from* the college, so increasing the sense of 'doing faith' and of 'being church', which may recall the inductive method of liberation theology. If so, the local ministry and the parish or congregation itself will have to accept greater responsibility for the growth of its ministry.

When members of a local congregation can see what is happening and are involved, they may be more willing to pay for what they 'own' and so help solve some of the cost problems of ministry development and the lack of stimulus. Hitherto, anxieties over costs have inhibited demand and, in turn, the supply of trained facilitators and tutors, and the institutional framework to support them. The typical college or diocesan development team, budgeted on a shoe-string, might then raise its sights. The substantial costs incurred by pre-ordination programmes for relatively small numbers of clergy are often in marked contrast to the very modest budgets which are 'left over' for post ordination or adult education programmes, which affect large numbers of people.

For almost all of the twenty Christian centuries, clergy have been educated to a more sophisticated level than members of the churches as a whole, thereby producing a clericalism which has disabled the 'laity'. Increasingly, professional support and development of the ordained clergy seems impoverished in comparison; the culture gap could well widen if nothing is done and the disabling happen in reverse.

The last decade has seen an immense drive into raising the promotion of quality management in industry and services, through such programmes as the Management Charter Initiative, National Council for Vocational Qualifications, British Standards 5750 or International Standard 9000, Investors in People, and Training and Enterprise Councils, Customer Charters. The result is an unprecedented level of organisational 'literacy' and awareness which makes many of the human transactions in churches look primitive.

Yet almost all the managerial/inter-personal/organisational processes and competences have their equivalents within the churches, albeit in a special context. Greater understanding will also promote a more acute judgement; there are many stories about clergy being too ready to accept the claims of consultants, whether paid or volunteers.

Indeed the churches might claim back the soundbite

language which industry has borrowed from religious contexts for the 'transformational' training of staff: 'envisioning', 'empowering for mission', 'credo', 'forgiveness' ... and put it to work with greater consistency where it belongs.

Evaluated to contribute to the effectiveness of ministry

Responding appropriately to changing circumstances presupposes a climate with greater willingness to monitor, evaluate and review *all* church activities than hitherto. Then a reflex to gauge the direction and effectiveness of ministry can become second nature and with it a habit of questioning and reviewing any system of professional support and development.

Measurement and analysis of faith activity are becoming more common. The first decennial census of church membership on a national scale was in 1979 but the government's national census due in 2001 does not yet have a religious question. Surveys of faith attitudes could be expanded through value questions within such opinion surveys as the annual British Social Attitudes Survey.[11]

Futures thinking or scenario planning is virtually unknown in a religious context, thereby inhibiting prospective planning. In industry, planning on the basis of past performance extrapolated has been likened to 'driving forwards by looking in the rear mirror'.[12]

Annual reports of dioceses and parishes and congregations could often be used to greater effect, not simply to recount what has been done, but to appraise achievements against aspirations and then to use the insights to plan for greater effectiveness in the future or changes of direction or emphasis in ministry.

At a congregational level, following the success of 'local church audits',[13] there have been suggestions that a variant of 'quality audits' might usefully be tried for some activities.[14] Naturally, all this must be done voluntarily in a spirit of inquiry; talk of central control and accountability might stifle enthusiasm. Hence, the concept of the 'learning organisation' which has been developing in secular management, ought to become habitual in the churches, particularly in respect of their ministries and therefore the shape of the evolving professional support and development needed.

The underlying prerequisite may be more understanding of faith activity as a *transaction*, something which is offered and satisfied. The suggestion of a transactional character may still generate pious objections. However, one of the special features of the Judaeo-Christian tradition is surely the 'transactional' nature of the relationship within the Trinity, between God and the people of God, and between me and my neighbour. Ministry is also a transaction, which needs to be felt, sensed, thought and intuited, and therefore evaluated so that professional support and development can be provided for.

Conclusions

In this chapter, we have sketched an approach to professional support and development which tries to be comprehensive and forward looking yet sensitive and flexible. The main argument is:

(a) a wider recognition of the 'professional' dimension of ministry;
(b) rooted in an organisational theology;
(c) which responds positively to its congregational context;
(d) and is part of a climate which is readier to evaluate faith activity;
(e) so that ordained clergy are animators of a learning and listening church.

NOTES

1. Eastell, Kevin (ed) *Appointed for Growth; a handbook for ministry development and appraisal* (Mowbray 1994).
2. Ministry to Priests Programmes of personal development are described briefly in Jacobs, Michael *Holding in Trust: the appraisal of ministry* SPCK 1989, and Kilroy, Bernard 'Priestly Development for Collaboration in Ministry' in *Doctrine and Life* Vol. 43 May/June 1993 No. 5, but a general assessment is long overdue.
3. Methodist Church *Accompanied Self-Appraisal* handbooks available direct from Division of Ministries, London NW1.

4. Unpublished material from URC, 86 Tavistock Place, London WC1.

5. Relevant explanatory leaflets available direct from Baptist Union, Didcot, Oxon.

6. Eastell op. cit. (p. 67).

7. General Synod House of Bishops *The Continuing Education of the Church's Ministers* GS Misc 122, 1980.

8. Apostolic Exhortation *Pastores Dabo Vobis* Catholic Truth Society 1990; Congregation for the Clergy *Directory on the Ministry and Life of Priests* CTS 1990; see also *Briefing* 18 July 1991 and 30 April 1992 of the RC Bishops' Conference of E & W.

9. Rudge, Peter F. *Management and Ministry* (1968 Tavistock) now out of print but remaining a key and in many ways unique inspiration, which is referred to elsewhere in the present book. Note that Rudge's book of 1976 is less conceptual. See also Kilroy, B. 'A Course in Managing Ministry' *Ministry* Edition 24 Winter 1994.

10. See in particular works by Avec's two previous coordinators: Lovell, George *Analysis and Design: a handbook for practitioners and consultants in church and community work* (Burns & Oates 1994; Widdecombe) Catherine *Group Meetings That Work: a practical guide* (St Pauls 1994) Avec's work in church consultancy ceased trading from premises in Chelsea in 1994 but an informal network continues. Other publications are obtaining from 'Resources', The Grail, Pinner.

11. *British Social Attitudes Survey* ed. Jowell R. and others published annually by Social and Community Planning Research.

12. see for instance Henry, Jane & Walker, David *Managing Innovation* Sage 1991.

13. Archbishop of Canterbury's Commission on Urban Priority Areas *Faith in the City* 1985 Church House (appendix A).

14. Cross ref to chapter 13.

16

Asking 'Why' questions now

MARTIN SEELEY

The surprising advice today to the churches from organisational management experts is, 'Do your theology!' It is no good to adapt old techniques or adopt new ones unless we are clear about the reasons for doing so, and that requires understanding our organisation's or group's basic purpose and identity. Asking the difficult 'why?' questions about purpose, meaning and values – questions about what we believe about ourselves – is seen as crucial as organisations seek to adjust and develop in a time of rapid social and economic change, without losing their essential identity and direction.[1]

Churches can engage with such 'why' questions when the issue concerns obvious and definable theological questions, such as those involved in liturgical change or the development of new patterns of ordained ministry. But when it comes to issues such as the church's management, regarded as less evidently theological, the tendency seems to be to devise a practice and then to construct a theological rationale. Many organisational theorists today would say this is the wrong way round. They would encourage us first to consider our purpose, who and what we are, why we exist, what we value and represent, what we do and why we do it. Only out of this process will we be able to develop practice suitable to engage with our changing needs and circumstances. If we lose sight of the 'why?' questions – the theological questions – our answers to the 'how?' questions will be built on sand – and quicksand at that.

171

Is this too daunting a prospect when we consider an institution like the Church of England? Not, these management specialists would say, if you encourage this process of enquiry in every level of the Church's life – the parish, diocese and national church, as well as in the organisations that contribute to the Church's work. Nor is this to suggest that 'why?' questions are the only questions to ask – nothing would happen if they were. But they are fundamental questions and need to be revisited from time to time in an era of major change.

In turning to the introduction of clergy appraisal, or ministerial review, in the Church of England, we can consider whether these 'why?' questions have been explored, and what consequences this might have had on the practices that have developed. In what ways and at what levels did the Church of England ask, 'what are our purpose and our values and in the light of these, why might ministerial review be a necessary or appropriate practice now?'

At a national level there seems to have been only a limited formal consideration of the appropriateness of ministerial review. Indeed, in 1984 the House of Bishops declined a recommendation that they study the emerging issue of clergy appraisal and assessment, although diocesan continuing ministerial education officers had discussed it at a conference in 1982 and a consultation was held at St George's House, Windsor in 1983 to consider it in relation to practice in industry and the armed forces. Only in July 1993 did the General Synod debate a diocesan motion urging bishops to implement a system of review and development for all clergy. By that time most dioceses had some sort of scheme in place.

So a remarkable burgeoning of schemes took place across dioceses, without consideration or prompting from the House of Bishops or General Synod. In 1980 just one diocese operated a procedure that might be identified as 'ministerial review'. In 1986 there were five with schemes in place while others were considering implementing one. Schemes then proliferated so that by 1990 they had been introduced in twenty-two dioceses – half the total – and by mid-1993 forty-one dioceses had adopted schemes. This rapid development had gained sufficient significance that in her 1991 novel, *The*

Rector's Wife, Joanna Trollope made two references to 'ministerial review'![2]

But what seems like a contagious process produced a remarkable diversity of types of schemes. In other areas, such as the provision of continuing ministerial education courses, dioceses exhibit a variety of practice, but this generally reflects a range of needs and resources in different dioceses, not a divergence of basic rationales. The question 'why?' has been considered sufficiently at a national and regional level to result in common elements of practice. When we consider diocesan ministerial review schemes, however, this does not seem quite the case. A survey of the tables in the appendices of 'Ministerial Review: Its Purpose and Practice'[3] shows not only that there are almost as many names for schemes as there are dioceses, but that no two schemes are alike. The variations are on quite basic lines, such as whether the review is conducted by or reported to the bishop and his staff, or is confidential to the reviewee and a peer reviewer; whether the scheme is voluntary or compulsory; whether reviews take place as frequently as once in six months, or as infrequently as once in three years. These basic differences suggest dioceses have generated very different responses to the questions of their own purpose and values and why they might undertake ministerial review. There is only limited evidence that dioceses have consulted with each other, and the consultation that has taken place seemed to be focused more on practice than rationale.

When we consider individual dioceses, the evidence suggests not all have thoroughly explored questions of their own purpose and values, and why review might be appropriate at this time. Several schemes clearly have been well-thought-out, carefully implemented, and are proving of value to both reviewees and their diocese. However, this seems not to be so in many dioceses. Officers from one diocese, reporting for 'Ministerial Review' disagreed about whether they even had a scheme! In other dioceses, officers reported objectives which differed from those outlined in the scheme's paperwork. Clergy have reported differences between what they believed their review was about and what they perceived the reviewer intended. No wonder Joanna Trollope can

describe the ministerial review scheme in *The Rector's Wife*
in one reference as 'diocesan checking-up' and in the other as
a 'care-of-priests scheme'.

Furthermore, many dioceses reported far more objectives
than seem reasonably achievable. For at least two-thirds of
the schemes more than five objectives were cited, and eleven
schemes indicated ten or more objectives. Some schemes in
which the reviewers are members of bishop's staff appear
unmanageable due to the number of reviews a reviewer is
expected to conduct. A scheme may include the expectation
that a bishop or archdeacon conduct fifty, sixty or seventy
reviews a year. Compared with the expectation of around
twelve in many 'secular' review programmes, this seems a
heavy demand, and it is clear several schemes are not working because of the workload. In other instances, the person
instrumental in conceiving the scheme may have considered
carefully why it was appropriate but had not engaged others
in the diocese in the same process of reflection. Schemes thus
produced by bishops or other diocesan officers have
collapsed when those key individuals have left or turned their
attention elsewhere.

Clearly a great deal of energy and hard work has gone into
developing and implementing ministerial review schemes in
the dioceses of the Church of England. This has been done
without, at a national level, a consideration of the Church's
purpose and values and whether ministerial review is necessary to their expression at this time. Such enquiry may have
occurred between some dioceses, but the evidence is slight.
Some individual dioceses may have considered the question,
but the ineffectiveness or unworkableness of schemes in
other dioceses suggests that has not been the case in all.

What spurred on this seemingly haphazard process? Was it
just the pressure to imitate other dioceses, or imitate 'secular'
institutions? Or was it a reaction to the increasing pace of
change in society and the Church? Change in the Church has
been felt strongly in recent years. In the late 1980s there was
growing concern about patterns of power and authority,
relationships between bishops, clergy and laity, and understandings of the ordained ministry and the nature and future
of the Church itself. Increasing financial pressures, the

change in the role of laity in the appointment of incumbents, and the prospect of the Synodical debate on the ordination of women, all contributed. The fundamental forces of money, power and sex were at work. Indeed, the preacher at the service for the opening of the new General Synod in 1950 began his sermon by declaring, ominously, 'We are assembled at a solemn time when the dogs of war are howling ever louder at our doors.[4]

If the dramatic development of ministerial review schemes was a response to such change in the Church, as well as to change in society, the question remains whether sufficient consideration has happened at a national level, or within and between dioceses, for this response to have been a creative and positive engagement with change, rather than a reaction against it. The 'why' questions must be asked. Is the Church of England provoking engagement with the vital theological questions about its purpose and values so that it has any chance of managing its life effectively in today's context of continuing upheaval?

NOTES

1. Discussion of this approach to organisational management can be found in such works as: Fullan, M., *Change Forces: Proving the Depths of Educational Reform* (London: The Falmer Press, 1993).
Senge, P., *The Fifth Discipline* (New York: Doubleday, 1990).
Swieringa, J., and Wierdsma, A., *Becoming a Learning Organization* (Workingham: Addison-Wesley, 1992).

2. Trollope, Joanna, *The Rector's Wife* (London: Bloomsbury, 1991); the two references to ministerial review are on pp. 71 and 256 of the paperback, Black Swan edition, 1992.

3. ABM Ministry Paper No. 6, *Ministerial Review: Its Purpose and Practice*. I served as secretary to the working party which produced this report.

4. The sermon was preached by Dr Henry Chadwick in Westminster Abbey on 13 November 1990.

17

Appraisal schemes

COLIN HILL

WHAT'S GOOD FOR THE ORGANISATION

Some of the Complexities

Firstly, a disclaimer: I have never organised nor been involved in implementing any form of staff appraisal scheme. At least I think that's right, but I'd better explain. As an Anglican clergyman I have been subject to ministerial review, but the ecumenical organisation with which I worked until recently, employing forty paid staff, hadn't seriously explored the possibility of a system of staff appraisal. I do, however, wonder if this is just a matter of terminology. We had various kinds of staff reviews associated with salary review, the completion of a probationary period of employment or the possible renewal of a contract. These were forms of 'appraisal' in that they were concerned with determining the value and effectiveness of individual performance.

We also had a system of supervision and support, derived and adapted from the worlds of social work and professional youth work. The only givenness about the scheme was that everyone in our organisation had someone with whom they could regularly share how things were going. The purpose of this was not to determine value, but to provide a context for individuals to reflect about the progress of their work and to share how they were feeling about it. For most staff, these meetings took place on a monthly basis. It was informal, in that it didn't involve set procedures, forms or reports. The 'supervisor' had questions such as:

'How are you?'
'How are things going (in general)?'
'What issues do you want to talk about?'
'How are things going in particular What about the things we talked about last time we met?'
'What things do you hope to achieve in the next little while?'

Did I say we didn't have an appraisal system? Well, we didn't in the sense that we had not adopted a formal staff appraisal scheme, but our practice was clearly one possibility amongst a whole range of procedures for supporting, encouraging, enabling, evaluating and, implicitly or explicitly, managing staff. I show what happened in our organisation, not because I have any desire at all to commend it or even to be content about it, but because it may illustrate the danger of thinking that staff appraisal is just one kind of formal procedure, or even two or three variations.

Frequently distinction is made between appraisal and personal review. Appraisal is to do with evaluating performance, whilst personal review is to do with personal and professional development. The distinction between 'sumative' appraisal, aimed at measuring achievements against some fixed standards, and 'formative' appraisal, based on consensual development, is also helpful. This was the distinction used by Dr Tony Berry in a paper delivered at a MODEM meeting in Manchester in 1994 (*Ministry* Spring 1995 p. 3). Another helpful distinction is that found in the Church of England's Advisory Board of Ministry Paper (January 1994) between hierarchical appraisal/review and peer appraisal/ review. This dichotomy focuses on who undertakes the review, but that also has implications for the nature and purpose of the exercise. There are other distinctions between different forms of appraisal. Are they, for example, concerned with management control or personal enablement; the achievement of team goals or personal job satisfaction; career development or accomplishing corporate objectives? So appraisal and review schemes are not one kind of procedure, they can vary enormously.

To add to the complexity, the church is, as John Nelson has pointed out, a rather distinctive organisation (*Ministry* Spring 1995). Considerable consequences flow from the subtly different roles of potential reviewers such as external consultants, 'fathers in God' (e.g. Bishops), managers (e.g. Archdeacons), senior colleagues (e.g. Rural Deans) and peers or soul mates. Few clergy have direct 'line managers' who are in touch with their day to day work (ABM 1994 p. 7). Church leaders, and Bishops in particular, are often acutely aware that they do not have the same direct control of staff which might be expected of managers, but they do have an extraordinarily powerful and deeply personal influence arising from the theological assumptions underlying their role (see ABM 1994 p. 41). These are important factors in deciding what will be appropriate in a church context.

Thus there are general questions about precisely what is meant by staff appraisal or personal review, and, added to this, are the particularities of the church. As if this were not enough there is also the considerable experience in secular organisations of ineffective appraisal schemes (Nelson, *Ministry* Spring 1995 p. 1). Although many secular appraisal schemes were initiated in order to try to introduce objectivity into an area where the idiosyncrasies of the judgement of managers can reign supreme, the effect is not always that intended. Organisations using formal appraisal schemes have sometimes been seen to offer even more opportunity for the subjective judgements and personal inclinations of managers to hold sway. There is even the opportunity for the development of 'reprisal schemes', with managers storing up information about real or imagined misdemeanours of staff, metaphorical payment for which is extracted via the 'next review'. That would, of course, be unthinkable for a professionally competent manager but the point is that appraisal schemes can provide the opportunity for the manipulation and undermining of staff just as readily for their encouragement, support and personal development. It is recognition of this which has led to the development of some extremely sophisticated appraisal schemes which contain elaborate checks and balances. Once such is the system of 'individual personal review' used in some parts of the National Health Service. This operates on a cycle of monitoring meetings and major performance reviews, is supported by comprehensive training on details of interpersonal relationship and involves the job holder, manager and 'grandparent' (the manager's manager). Information is not available regarding the long-term effectiveness of this particular scheme, but the thoroughness and detail of the scheme depends on the avail-ability of sophisticated resources which are well beyond the means of any major English church denomination. Given that the church is not in the position to develop the scheme with such a range of checks and balances to guard against abuse, then clarity about the precise purpose of the exercise is even more critical.

There are three fundamental agendas which could be addressed by a scheme of appraisal or review: firstly, personal development and job satisfaction of the individual; secondly, the personal performance and career development of the individual; and thirdly, the achievement of the corporate goals of the organisation. These are clearly inter-related, but they are not the same.

Organisational Development and Appraisal/Review/Affirmation

It is the achievement of the corporate goals of the organisa-tion with which the next part of this chapter is concerned.

Some very general aims might be identified as applying to all organisations. For example, almost any organisation, ecclesiastical or otherwise, might have three aims: firstly to accomplish its specific purpose, or, to put it another way, realise its 'mission statement'. Secondly, in this modern world, it may wish to accomplish this at minimum cost. Thirdly, it may want to do so in such a way as to be flexible enough to respond to changing situations and circumstances. However generalised and obvious these aims might be, there is still a significant danger of church organisations being diverted by the displacement objectives. That is to say, the organisation is in fact working towards some other set of purposes, either secondary or even totally unacknowledged, rather than its primary stated purposes. Thus, a church which is too dominated by treasurers and financial managers may actually be aiming at financial success more than anything else. Neither is it unheard of for a church to appear to be organised entirely for the personal fulfilment of the clergyman! Ineffective commercial organisations have sometimes found that their real problem has been their total preoccupation with management control rather than producing the best product, at minimum cost and with maximum responsiveness to market changes. Church organisations are not always exempt from this accusation!

So, in thinking about the church organisation, let's assume that it has an agreed 'mission statement' and that the purpose of the organisation is to accomplish this at minimum financial cost and with maximum responsiveness to changes in external circumstance. Let's also assume a high level of self awareness about displaced objectives and about dangers of appraisal/review schemes being tailored for the personal satisfaction of managers and quasi-managers. Leavitt claims that four factors govern the development of an organisation: task, technology, organisation structure and people (Leavitt, 1965) I would add a fifth, financial resources. Organisations can become fixated on any of these: 'all we really need is a new computer system'; 'the real problem is a lack of accountability between the different boards'; 'if only we had enough money!'. As, however, Margerison puts it 'the essence of organisation development is the extent to which people are prepared and able to change' (Margerison, 1973 p. 213). So the challenge is to create conditions such that people will embrace change.

The church has a tendency to look longingly at secular organisations, sure that they must have something to teach. They have, but it's not all good. In one study, none of the managers' 'behaviour was of the type to encourage human and organisation development. They did not invite others to share their responsibilities, nor did they develop a co-operative relationship and did not present opportunities for others to take initiative and assume new responsibilities.' (Argyris, 1973). Many modern and successful industrial organisations have taken this kind of indictment very seriously, hence programmes such as 'investors in people'. These recognise the individuals who constitute the work force as the company's major asset.

Thus the question arises as to how to motivate staff. As

early as the mid 1960s there was clear evidence about this. In one survey the two top factors characterising job satisfaction were: achievement and recognition. The top two factors characterising dissatisfaction were: company policy and supervision. (Herzberg 1968) Similar results are quoted by Nicholson. The three most prized features of employment for a group of workers were: full appreciation of work done; a feeling of being involved and knowing what was going on and, thirdly, job security. (Nicholson, 1992 p. 63). Clergy, and other workers for churches and Christian organisations, will have other motives and sources of job satisfaction. These will be matters of religious vocation and personal belief. They may be very powerful in their influence, but they do not stop church employees being human and being affected by matters of human motivation very much like other people. The division between 'extrinsic' and 'intrinsic' motivators is helpful here (Nicholson, 1992 p. 63). 'Extrinsic' motivators are the financial rewards, physical working conditions, holidays, material fringe benefits and the like. It is not unreasonable to assume that religious motivations dramatically modify the importance of these extrinsic factors for people like clergy. 'Intrinsic' motivators include a friendly organisation, a sense of purpose, feelings of knowing what is happening and being appreciated. Religious motivations could well be included in this classification. Furthermore, it could be argued that religious motivations actually enhance the significance of intrinsic factors, they are so inextricably bound up with them. Some one who has given up well paid job prospects in order to work for the church may well expect to be 'appreciated' even more than someone who is being very well paid. Whatever the case, people across a range of employment areas cite the intrinsic items far more than the extrinsic ones when saying why they like their work (Nicholson, 1992 p. 63).

So, to return to the development of the organisation: for the organisation to maximise its potential, staff need to be motivated, and the keys to this, especially in religious organisations, are intrinsic factors. A system of appraisal/review could play a powerful and positive part. It also could be very unhelpful, it if has the effect of making staff feel bad about themselves. To achieve the organisation's objectives, minimise cost and be flexible and responsive, a number of features will need to characterise the staff and how they work. These include the following:

(a) ability to innovate
(b) open communications
(c) high self value
(d) clarity about goals
(e) participatory style
(f) 'bottom up' initiatives
(g) self awareness

If the staff appraisal/review scheme is to nurture these, it must be fundamentally about affirmation and space to reflect. It must not be about evaluation and the threat of censure. This implies a separation of management control from personal review. It does not imply the kind of self-indulgent navel gazing to which clergy can fall prey. Churches and church organisations have jobs to do. They need to be clear about their objectives and tasks, and not to expend all their staff energies on introspection. To do this, staff need to feel positive about themselves, and the organisation for which they work, and liberated and energised to contribute to the corporate objectives. This is all very obvious, and yet, of the 50 Church of England Diocesan appraisal/review schemes surveyed by ABM, only 26 included 'provide pastoral care, support, affirmation and/or encouragement' amongst their published objectives. On the other hand, 35 schemes had objectives which included 'review a person's ministry, usually against criteria such as derived from the ordinal, or previously set objectives'. (ABM, 1994 p. 36f). An immense amount of thought and care, and genuine concern for the well being of clergy, has gone into the development of these schemes, yet evaluating against criteria still predominates over affirming and supporting amongst the published objectives of the schemes.

The name of the scheme is important. The title 'Appraisal', with its connotation of seeing if people are up to standard, is probably unhelpful. I am not too sure if 'a review' is much better. Church of England Dioceses have clearly been very sensitive to the importance of the name of the scheme. On the range of titles used, 'Support in Ministry' (Manchester) and 'Sounding Board' (Peterborough) are amongst those giving the clearest signals about affirmation of clergy.

The frequency of meetings in the scheme may be similarly significant. If a scheme is about encouragement then an interview every year, or even more frequently, might give better signals than one every three years, seen, as it well could be, as a major event with all the associated stress. The same is true of forms and formalities: they tend to heighten stress and make people defensive.

In case you think that all I have in mind is a cosy fire-side chat, then let me comment on the role of the interviewer. Those implementing the scheme aimed at liberating staff energies and creativity will need a significant level of skill in perceiving what the interviewee is saying, verbally and non-verbally. Alongside this they will need a high level of self-awareness, so that their own needs and priorities do not take over control of the interview. One of the most reassuring facts to emerge from the ABM survey of dioceses is the high proportion of schemes in which the 'reviewers' received both initial and on-going training.

Summary

In this brief chapter I have drawn attention to the variety of staff appraisal/review schemes, their openness to abuse and the need for clarity of purpose in divising and implementing a scheme. I suggested three basic purposes for such schemes: personal development and job satisfaction; personal performance and career development; the achievement of corporate goals. I then focused on organisational development.

The organisation needs not only to be clear about its own objectives but also clear about the importance of motivating people. The importance of intrinsic, as opposed to extrinsic, motivating factors was noted. I again pointed to the need to separate management control from staff affirmation. Details of a scheme such as name, frequency of interview and associated formalities are important in the signals they give to those interviewed. I then concluded with reference to the demands made on the interviewer.

This has not been intended as a technical analysis of staff appraisal schemes, but reflections on the needs of churches and church bodies for their organisational development. Summative staff appraisal schemes have their place, but we must be clear that their purpose is to evaluate individual performance and exercise management control. Schemes such as these are, on their own, unlikely to maximise the organisation's potential for development. What I advocate here is a style of staff support and system of affirmation which will, if sufficient attention is given to detail and self awareness of those implementing it, contribute very significantly to organisational development.

REFERENCES

Advisory Board of Ministry of the Church of England *Ministerial Review: its Purpose and Practice.*

ABM Ministry Paper No. 6 January 1984.

Central Board of Finance of the Church of England 1994.

Argyris, C. 'The C.E.O.'s Behaviour Key to Organisational Development' Harvard Business Review, March/April 1973.

Herzberg, F. 'How Do You Motivate Employees' Harvard Business Review January/February 1968.

Leavitt, H. G. 'Applied Organisation Change in Industry' in *A Handbook of Organisations* (Edited J March (Rand McNally 1965).

Margerison, C. J *Organisational Development – A Managerial Problem Solving Approach.* A Management Decision Making Monograph, Volumem 11 No. 4, Summer 1973, MCB Ltd.

Ministry: Journal of Edward King Institute for Ministry Development and MODEM, Edition No. 25, Spring 1995.

National Health Service Training Authority *Knowledge Book: IPR Making it Work* PDA Consulting Group Ltd 1987.

Nicholson, J. *How Do You Manage* (BBC Books, London 1992).

18

Human resource management

BRYAN PETTIFER

The management of people is as essential to the life of the church as it is to the life of any organisation. In this chapter the Church of England's policy in the management of people will be examined from the perspective of the theory and practice of human resource management. The development of human resource management will be sketched briefly and some of its main characteristics identified in Section 1. The relation of the human resource management perspective to a theological understanding of the Church will be discussed in Section 2. Some of the main themes of human resource management will be explored in relation to the Church in Section 3. In Section 4 a changing paradigm of ministry will be discussed and, finally, there will be consideration of the role of the centre.

1. Strategic Human Resource Management

Human resource management is a comparatively recent development within the tradition of personnel management.[1] The latter is a more general term still used widely in the literature and in practice. It is probably best to understand human resource management (HRM) as a normative model of personnel management. Therefore, a brief history of the development of personnel management may provide useful background information.

Torrington and Hall[2] suggest that in the history and literature of the subject a number of models of the personnel

187

manager may be found and that elements of each of them are still to be found in current practice. The first model was the **social reformer** who fought for working people who were degraded and dehumanized by working conditions in the early days of the Industrial Revolution. Their work led to the first appointments of personnel managers. The second model was the **welfare officer** who dispensed benefits to the deserving and unfortunate employees and where the employer's motivation was Christian charity. Elements of this strand in the tradition can still be seen where personnel departments care for dependents of employees and former employees. The third model is the **humane bureaucrat,** where organisational rather than paternalistic employee relations come more to the fore. In this model personnel officers will deal with staffing, selection, and training matters and through it the organisation shows its concern for good industrial relations and employee morale. The fourth model is the **consensus negotiator** which adds to the previous mix the function of bargaining over wages and conditions of service. Among clergy the absence of significant unionisation so far means that this has not been prominent within the Church. However the recent Anglican report on Clergy Conditions of Service has given it a higher profile. The fifth model is the **organisation man**. In this the focus shifts away from employee relations to an emphasis on individuals especially managers and their development. In a more competitive world the relationship of the organisation to its environment is given greater emphasis. The sixth model is the **manpower analyst**. With rising payroll costs from the seventies onwards, the utilisation and improvement of an organisation's human resources became more central to the organisation's strategic planning.

In the model of HRM many of the themes and concerns in previous models are taken up but there are significant changes of emphasis. The emphasis in HRM is to treat people as an asset rather than seeing them just as a cost. With this goes a responsibility for gaining the greatest return on those assets and it is a responsibility shared by all managers and not just those in the personnel department. HRM has a more co-operative ethos compared with the directive ethos of manpower planning. There is a growing realisation that people cannot be treated like other resources. The needs, expectations and values which motivate them need to be understood and respected.

There are four further characteristics of HRM. The first is an emphasis on the importance of culture, including the values, organisational climate, and management style which affect the quality of the organisation's work. This includes a sense that culture is something which needs to be managed and exemplified from the top. The second is an emphasis on developing a common sense of purpose and a shared commitment to change in pursuit of that purpose. The third is the way people are treated as individuals by their line managers and how the organisation expresses this in its personnel policies and procedures. This attitude to employees is seen as important in achieving the mission and strategic goals of the organisation. Fourthly and perhaps the most important aspect of HRM is the way in which it provides a strategic basis for personnel policies and uses them to further that organisation's mission.

In the HRM literature a distinction is sometimes made between 'hard' and 'soft' HRM. 'Hard' HRM will ensure that the organisation 'has the right numbers of the right people in the right places at the right time',[3] and resource utilisation and cost minimalisation will be important concerns. 'Soft' human resource management is much broader and is more concerned with defining where the organisation is at present and how it should be changing to meet its mission goals in the future. It is concerned with relating the organisation to its environment and to important trends and changes which are taking place in the world where it is set. It is concerned with employee development with enabling and empowering employees to take more responsibility for operations, quality and adaptability, with reshaping the organisational culture and with the management of change. Human resource management is more prescriptive than descriptive and presents a perceived ideal of how to manage the organisation's human resources.

Yet in many industrial and commercial organisations the ideal is not being fulfilled. In the multi-divisional company where a number of distinct enterprises are controlled and largely owned by a central body, the process called portfolio planning takes place. Constituent divisions or companies are evaluated from the centre purely in terms of their financial yield and human resource management is only seen to be of significance if the financial yield, often viewed in a very short term perspective, can be seen to benefit. In these circumstances human resource management may be an ideal which has little impact or indeed is a virtual non-starter.[4]

The ideals of human resource management may be more relevant and attainable in relation to the Church than to industrial and to commercial organisations. The development of persons is not just a means to a financial end but one of the ends which is central to its mission. The financial affairs of the Church are not dominated by the profit issue. On the other hand the Church is not always seen as a good employee, benevolent intentions are often combined with a lack of understanding of, and insight into, personnel management issues and inadequate skills and experience for handling them. The Church of England is very decentralised and so much of the management of people takes place within dioceses and, therefore, there is a variety of practices. The relation between dioceses and central structures is to be considered further in Section 5.

2.   Theology and Human Resource Management

The Church is wise not to embrace contemporary disciplines of thought and practice unquestioningly. For example, from the fifties onwards pastoral care suffered from taking into its systems the methods and assumptions of various models of counselling without critically appraising them. For the Church a theological critique will be central but it needs to work in partnership with philosophical, ethical, sociological and psychological critiques. In the following paragraphs, two examples will be given of how theology and HRM might be related. The first is by examining the assumptions about persons which are implicit in HRM and comparing this with how the Church's beliefs about persons are or are not reflected in the way it handles its human resources. The second illustration is how theology relates to the task of managing a firm's corporate culture especially its values.

Embedded deep in HRM is a higher degree of respect for persons than was found in earlier models of personnel management. Employees are valued more for themselves and their development is seen as something worth investing in. Training and development therefore become more important. Appraisal is seen as a key tool in stimulating development. A more co-operative and less competitive management style is preferred. These emphases produce a dividend; they help to maintain a firm's competitive advantage. This is usually maintained by a combination of the firm's resources of skills and its culture of routines which use the the skills to their best advantage. At the end of the day the purpose of it is to maintain the firm's market position and profits.

Respect for persons is a basic assumption without which talk of Christian love becomes meaningless. The Church's mission is more person-centred than any commercial organisations, at least in theory, but how is this actually worked out in practice? Developing as persons and developing our discipleship go together as we grow in the knowledge and love of God, and worship will contribute to this. For some members of congregations worship goes on week by week but the pastoral care and fellowship do little to nurture their development in other ways. An example of this may sometimes be seen in a choir. Choir and organist are valued for their music but their broader development can be neglected over a long period of time so that they become rigid and inflexible factors in the Church's life, resisting change which is essential to the Church's mission. Music may be a person's principal gift but is not the totality of who they are. There is a further question to be asked about the next stage in the development of these people as part of the human resources of the Church.

It has already been indicated above that 'soft' HRM involves managing the corporate culture, especially its values. Sometimes its values are expressed in normal routines and patterns of behaviour, in its style of management, in its relationship to customers of the firm, and the quality of the product. To manage the corporate culture, therefore, requires integrating the various core values that belong to the organisation. The Church's values are articulated through its theology but there is a task focusing and integrating the theology, beliefs and values for the whole Church. In a church which has been increasingly split into party groupings with their own sub-cultures, it is vital to recover those things which hold the Church of England together, the values which we all share. Central to this is the rediscovery of the symbolic role of a National Church for the nation.

In applying the theory of HRM to the Church, the assumptions built into it need to be evaluated from a theological perspective. The Church is an organisation centred round a theology rather than a profit motive and, therefore, its theology will be crucial in understanding its organisational structure and purpose.

3.   Managing the Church's Human Resources

Some dominant themes in HRM will be presented and related to the Church in this section. The first theme is **mission** which is a word widely used by organisations today and was, of course, originally borrowed from the Church. Mission statements are found to be useful in clarifying an organisation's purpose. Its various activities are integrated by relating a more specific aim to its central task as defined in its mission statement. In the Church there has been plenty of writing from the New Testament onwards about the mission of the Church but thinking in this field is less well focused than in organisations with a more specific task. There is also a diversity of views about how the mission of the Church should be conceived in our present context.

HRM is commonly qualified with the adjective strategic to indicate the crucial importance of integrating HRM policies and business strategies. Business strategy and human resource strategy are conceived as being ways in which the organisation's mission is pursued and harmonising them is the goal of the second theme, **strategic integration**. This means ensuring a good fit between mission strategy and the management of human resources. For the church it means developing relations between clergy and laity in a way which increases co-operation and participation.

The third HRM theme is theoretical coherence so that the various policies, methods and techniques adopted by a firm in the field of HRM are chosen and used in a co-ordinated way to improve organisational effectiveness. In general this means that each of the main 'people management' interventions, selection, appraisal, rewards and development contribute to a common goal. More especially ideas such as organisation development, career planning, job enrichment, performance related pay, etc. are not adopted piecemeal and used in isolation but are implemented as part of a coherent human resource strategy. Thus in the Church, lay training, adult catechumenate, appraisal, stewardship of talents, etc., should not be taken up one by one as being in turn the new answer to all the Church's problems. They should each be evaluated in terms of individual needs and the requirements of the Church and introduced as part of a coherent policy to develop people in the Church and to equip them to play their part in its mission.

The concept of the flexible firm has been prominent in recent HRM literature. This is about **flexibility in the managing of people and also flexibility in responding to the needs of mission**. Many organisations are moving towards a structure which is flexible in having a core of permanent members, some of whom might be part-time, but in which a substantial amount of work is done by subcontractors, outworkers, seasonal and temporary staff, which allows the possibility of the firm expanding or contracting as the market changes. With it has gone a move away from a collective emphasis in the management of the workforce to an individualistic one. By contrast the Church of England has a stipendiary workforce in which two-thirds of the clergy have a freehold which makes it far less flexible than other organisations, or indeed, than other churches. This issue is being addressed through the Clergy Conditions of Service Steering Group set up by the General Synod. Many clergy are feeling insecure and therefore hold on to the security of the freehold. They are a vital resource for the Church as part of its permanent work force. Ways need to be found, on the one hand, to ensure them of their permanent place in the Church without the rigidity of the freehold and, on the other hand, to increase the flexibility of their deployment in the service of the Church's mission.

The **management of change** is increasingly seen as a component part of all management including HRM. Many levers of change in the Church of England are being pulled simultaneously. The Archbishops' Commission on the Organisation of the Church of England (Turnbull Commission), a Review of Synodical Government, the Review of Clergy Conditions of Service, a Review of Cathedrals are all potentially very important change agents. Many dioceses are reviewing their pastoral strategies. Amidst so much ferment many people are holding on more tightly to the status quo. However, at the same time, change is taking place in a positive and creative way at all levels of church life. The section which follows identifies a possible direction for change in the Church's management of people.

Finally HRM puts great emphasis upon **commitment** by enabling people to identify with the mission goals and core values of the organisation. An important task is to integrate the needs of the organisation with the needs of the individual. It is a participative approach in order to unleash the latent creativity and energy of the people in it. Part of the secret of managing change is to enable people to own the direction of change.

There are a variety of concepts of HRM and many ways in which it could be related to church life. The themes from HRM, selected for discussion above, and the way they have been related to issues in church life are illustrative of how the church may be seen in the perspective of HRM.

4.   A New Paradigm of Ministry?

In the Church of England, and especially in the work of the House of Bishops, attention has been given to man and woman power planning. There has been a preoccupation with declining numbers of stipendiary ministers and more recently an anxiety that the financial resources might not be available to support the ministers it has. If numbers declined further it was questioned whether they could still do the same job in Church and nation which they had hitherto done. However this seems to assume that clergy roles are remaining static:

The management of change in ministry cannot be viewed simply in terms of stipendiary ministers. Anglican clergy are and have been a notable feature of British life, with so many distinctive characteristics. But the human resources of the Church are predominantly lay people and they have been contributing more and more to the life and ministry of the Church, not just in terms of the practical needs of the Church and in its administration and democracy but in a variety of other kinds of ministry.

The result is that a quiet revolution is already underway in many places. The task of the clergy in preaching, leading worship, teaching, pastoral care, etc., is more and more widely shared. This often develops under the leadership of wise imaginative and forward looking clergy but may be shortlived and revert when clergy leadership changes.

In conversation with a theological college principal it was suggested that this 'paradigm shift' in the role of the stipendiary clergy was the way forward. This was accepted as though it could be taken as read and yet the implications are not fully worked out for the initial training of clergy, still less for continuing ministerial education, nor is such a shift significantly reflected in the pastoral strategy documents produced by dioceses. In the recruitment and selection process the pervasive influence of earlier role models remains powerful.

This 'paradigm shift' and the consequent redefinition of the clerical role could become a central component in a new strategy for ministry. In a discussion of the management of change in which it is stressed that it is important to begin with the knowledge and attitude of individuals it has been stated 'individual behaviour is powerfully shaped by the organisational roles that people play. The most effective way to change behaviour, therefore, is to put people into a new organisational context which imposes new roles, responsibilities and relationships on them.'[6] The suggestion that is being made here is that a new organisational context is not being imposed but is gradually emerging in the life of the Church, though very erratically. What is needed is a clear and consistent policy of implementing this paradigm shift.

The Epistle to the Ephesians sees the responsibility of a number of ministries, listed in 4.11 apostles, prophets, evangelists, pastors and teachers, as being two-fold. It is 'to equip God's people for work in his service' and 'to build up the body of Christ'. This puts a heavy stress upon the responsibility of the Church's special ministers for the human resource development and management of all God's people.

Clergy have a management task but it is very unlike management in large organisations staffed by paid employees. It is more like the management role carried out by paid organisers in voluntary bodies which in themselves are largely led by unpaid volunteers. This is a style of management which requires a very high level of skill. The essential change is from a role of ministry and leadership to a much greater emphasis upon the oversight of others who are ministering and leading. The word for oversight in the New Testament is episcope and traditionally this has been a function of Bishops. However, for centuries in the Church of England it has been delegated at local level to stipendiary clergy. In the words of the institution charge 'your care my cure' in which the Bishop's responsibility for the pastoral care of the parish is delegated to the parish priest by entrusting him or her with the 'cure of souls', a legal term for the priest's role in the parish.

This change which is already partial reality needs to be developed much more systematically. It could have the effect of liberating lay people to find new opportunities in the life of the Church. It would require redefinition of the task of the clergy in relation to a developing emphasis upon mission and would require a clearer recruitment policy so that the Church attracted the kind of clergy it will need to implement a new strategy. The emphasis will be much more on the quality of stipendiary ministers rather than of their quantity. There would also need to be changes in the role of Bishops and Archdeacons, especially in their relationship to stipendiary clergy.

5. Rediscovering the Role of the Centre

The structure of the Church of England is decentralised in the sense that many issues of policy are decided by dioceses independently of each other. On the other hand it is sometimes argued that the centre is too costly and should be radically reduced in size. At a time when proposals for restructuring the Church of England's central resource management are being considered there is a need to ask what the function of the centre should be. In multi-divisional companies, the centre usually exerts strong central control over the profitability of the divisions and HRM may be largely delegated down to the divisions. However, there has been also a rediscovering of the tasks of the centre and five tasks which are relevant to the Church will be considered in this section.

Firstly, the centre generally has an opportunity to exercise cultural leadership by focusing the theology, beliefs and values for the whole Church. This means **articulating and integrating the core values** that belong to a common organisation however dispersed and decentralised its structure is. In Section 2 we have already referred to the urgent and fundamental need to discover the symbolic function of a national church for the nation as a whole especially as the bearer of values. There is a more specific symbolic role for its ordained leaders and this has important implications for their recruitment, selection, training and continuing development. Regardless of churchmanship differences the nation has expectations of the Church which the latter ignores at its peril.

Second, the centre will still need to be involved in **human resource planning** especially in relation to the shared resources of ordained ministry. An organisation's core values should determined how it recruits, selects, trains and appraises. The paradigm shift in the Church's ministry proposed in the previous section would affect how each of these functions was carried out.

The third task of the centre is to **build on the 'synergies'** which may be defined as follows: 'synergy is what happens when the combined performance of a company's resources is greater than the sum of its parts'.[5] Becoming the people of

God and the body of Christ means that the full potential of laity and clergy is realised. It means being in Christ, living in the power of the Spirit and living by the grace of our Lord Jesus Christ. A prayer requests the Holy spirit to impart to us 'thoughts higher than our own thoughts, powers beyond our own powers'. In *The Alternative Service Book 1980* after communion we pray 'May we who share Christ's body live his risen life; we who drink his cup bring life to to others; we whom the spirit lights give life to the world'. But how is this synergy to be realised? The previous section suggested that a paradigm shift in the management of the Church's human resources would make a major contribution to the development of synergy by using the lay and clerical resources of the Church more effectively.

Fourthly, the centre can **encourage innovation** and enable different parts of the Church to learn from each other. There is a vital need to monitor new initiatives in order to communicate good practice between parishes and between dioceses.

Finally, central bodies can make possible **economies of scale**. Forty-four dioceses replicating the same structures can be wasteful and, in certain tasks, such as training, especially continuing ministerial education for stipendiary ministers, for example, a regional structure could be much more effective.

Conclusion

This chapter has argued that strategic human resource management offers a useful perspective from which to view the life of the Church. Although there are many models or concepts of HRM available it has been possible to make connections with church life by relating to it some common themes in HRM. The Church's use of HRM theory requires an appropriate theological critique. The Church is, in some respects, in a transitional phase in which a redefinition of the role of stipendiary clergy and the gradual opening up of ministry to lay people are taking place. Together they are indicative of a paradigm change in ministry and this change needs to be focused as matter of policy and built into the Church's strategic thinking. Related to this is the need to rediscover the role of the centre.

It has been an exercise in practical theology, which requires drawing on both the resources of the Christian tradition and the insights of a secular discipline, in this case HRM, in order to re interpret the experience of the Church and to make it more effective in its mission.

NOTES

1. Among the sources used in writing this chapter are the following:
   Armstrong, M. and Long, P. *The Reality of Strategic HRM*, IPD, 1994.
   Armstrong, M. Ed. *Strategies for Human Resource Management*, Kogan Page, 1992.
   Purcell, J. and Ahlstrand, B. *Human Resource Management in Multi-divisional Company* OUP, 1994.
   Sisson, K. ed. *Personnel Management* Blackwell, 1994.
   Storey, J. ed. *New Perspectives on Human Resource Management*, Routledge, 1989.
   Storey, J. *New Developments in the Management Human Resources*, Blackwell, 1992.
   Storey, J. ed. *Human Resource Management: A Critical Text* Routledge, 1994.
   Torrington, D. and Hall, L. *Personnel Management Second Edition*, Prentice Hall International UK Limited, 1991.
   In exploring HRM literature I would like to acknowledge the help of John Purcell, Thom Watson, David Perry and Ian Pettifer.

2. Torrington and Hall. op. cit. pp. 4–9.

3. Torrington and Hall, op. cit. p. 49.

4. Further discussion of this see Purcell, J. 'The Impact of Corporate Strategy on Human Resource Management' in Storey 1989 and Purcell, J. 'Corporate Strategy and Human Resource Management' in Storey 1994.

5. Armstrong, 1994, p. 8.

6. Beer, M. Eisenstat, R. and Spector, B. 1990 'Why Change Programmes don't Produce Change', *Harvard Business Review* November/December. Quoted in Armstrong 1992 p. 23.

19

Information technology in church mission and strategy

GARETH G. MORGAN

(This chapter is an adaptation of a paper Dr Gareth Morgan presented at the MODEM One-Day Conference on 'Appropriate Information Technology to Support the Management of the Church' held at York University in June 1995, and parts of it have been previously published in the article 'ITEM: A Strategic Approach to Information Systems in Voluntary Organisations' included in the *Journal of Strategic Information Systems* 4(3) 1995, copyright Elsevier Science BV, and are used with permission.)

The notions of mission statements and parish audits are now becoming reasonably accepted in UK churches, but it is rare to see examples of specific decisions following from these on practical issues like information technology (IT). Where IT is used in local churches it is often on a haphazard basis with little contribution to the overall mission and strategy of the church. This chapter reports some detailed case study research carried out in ten local churches leading to the development of the ITEM approach which seeks to enable a church to devise and implement an IT strategy appropriate to its own sense of mission. It is argued that the effective use of IT in churches is only possible when set in the context of a doctrine of the church that takes seriously the stewardship of information.

1.   Notions of Organisational Mission in Local Churches

It is now widely accepted that for organisations of all kinds to be effective in their work they need to engage in the process of strategic management. Whilst the modern emphasis on organisational strategy derives mainly from work in commercial organisations, particularly large ones,[1] it is clearly seen as a discipline that is relevant to organisations of all sizes.

Moreover, it can be argued that in churches and charities, which by definition exist for reasons other than financial profit, the need for defining organisational strategy is even greater – because a non-profit organisation stands a greater risk of being distracted from its main task if its strategy is unclear.

Defining Organisational Strategy

These issues have seen a considerable acceptance in church contexts in the last ten years or more, and several publications have emerged seeking to help churches define their strategy: their vision, and their priorities for action,[2] although such ideas are by no means new.[3]

Most writers accept a need to define strategy at several levels, and although some very complex schemes have been proposed, it is sufficient for the purpose here to consider just three levels:

(a)   A statement of *organisational mission*. This is a relatively short statement (many suggest it should not exceed 50 words) which sums up what the organisation exists for. Although the word 'mission' meets some objections in a commercial context it is highly appropriate when applied to churches, as most churches will readily accept that their existence has something to do with 'mission' in the broadest sense.

(b)   From the mission statement, an organisation requires some *statements of organisational objectives*. These spell out in broad terms the main tasks or areas of work that the organisation intends to undertake: they show how the mission statement will be put into effect. It is here that churches need to be selective: no church can do everything, and each church must identify its main areas of strategic action.

(c) From the broad organisational objectives must emerge some clear statements of *specific goals*. These define particular measurable targets which the organisation is committed to achieving within a specific timescale. If strategy is to mean anything it must be possible to monitor how well the strategy is being achieved, and that is impossible without measurable goals.

The use of such language is not acceptable to all in church work, and some of the publications mentioned use terminology with a more obviously Christian flavour. Moreover, even in the specific case of local churches, writers such as Rudge[4] have shown that there are at least five distinct models of church organisation, each of which has different notions of organisational strategy. But the basic need for churches to have a clear sense of parish mission is now very widely accepted, and many Anglican dioceses, for example, are now requiring each parish to come up with its own mission statement, spelling out its priorities.

This has been greatly strengthened by the notion of parish audits, first widely suggested in the report *Faith in the City*.[5] Such audits challenge churches to identify with reasonable accuracy the composition of their parishes and resources available or lacking, so that a church may plan its own strategy based on a proper understanding of the community it is seeking to serve. This is an example of the churches taking up the principle that strategy formulation must be preceded by appropriate strategic analysis, especially analysis of the organisation's environment.

Using Organisational Strategy

The concept of organisational strategy is that once defined it becomes *the basis of all other major decisions*.

For example when questions are faced about expenditure on the church building, or changing the pattern of ministry, or launching new groups within the church, the church

council (or appropriate decision making body) can avoid
having to start from first principles when making each
decision, with the possible result that different decisions
are taken with different long term objectives in mind. Rather,
the principle is that each question is addressed from the
standpoint of asking: which solution will best support our
overall mission?

In principle this should mean that over a period of time a
range of decisions are taken, each of which in different ways
supports the overall mission, and thus the church gradually
becomes much more focused on its central task. The process
is not static, and the mission needs to be periodically redefined on an iterative basis (particularly the short term goals).

However, it is suggested by the present author that even
where churches have taken the time to develop a notion of
their own mission and strategy, far too few decisions are
taken on that basis. The use and application of IT is a classic
example where even churches which appear to have a very
strong notion of long term vision can find they have totally
failed to take any kind of strategic view in the way they have
gone about using IT.

This chapter seeks to offer some way forward on this
problem, and proposes a possible approach by which a
church can be enabled to devise and implement an IT strategy which directly supports the church's overall mission.

2.   Patterns of I.T. Usage in churches – The Need for I.T. Strategy

The use of IT in churches and small voluntary organisations
has increased greatly in the last 12 years with the advent of
personal computers (PCs). But numerous authors have
argued that the use of IT in this sector is often haphazard,
poorly planned, and inadequately related to the needs of the
organisation.[6]

To those accustomed to more substantial uses of IT, the
patterns of use in churches can seem extremely primitive.
Very few local churches possess more than a single PC, a
printer, and some suitable software packages. As well as
general purpose applications such as word processing,

spreadsheets and desk top publishing, many are also using software, specifically developed for church and voluntary organisations, to cover areas such as membership records, charitable accounting, stewardship schemes, and reclaiming tax on deeds of covenant.[7] However, at the more advanced end, some larger church offices have invested in local area networks with perhaps four machines, and some churches are using facilities for external data communications by access to electronic mail facilities through Internet providers.

In addition to equipment owned by the church, there may well be further hardware and software owned by individual ministers and lay people which they use, in some cases extensively, in relation to the work of the church. For example, it is not uncommon to find that the minister has a personal word processor, and that the treasurer has access to a PC with a spreadsheet, even though neither is under the church's own control. In determining an IT strategy, careful account must be taken of such systems. Dependence on personally-owned equipment can leave a church very vulnerable if there are personnel changes, but ignoring it can lead to new computer systems being ineffective, if individuals prefer to continue with their own personal facilities.

If the church has a permanently staffed office, that will be the natural location for the church's own hardware, but church offices are still largely the preserve of well-resourced urban parishes. However, as in other voluntary organisations, much church work is carried out by volunteers, often in their evenings and weekends, and it may not be convenient or possible for them to have to go into an office for access to IT facilities. Thus it is not uncommon to find equipment purchased by the church but located in the home of (say) the treasurer. The location of the hardware is a major issue in determining its effective use.

Also, regardless of ownership, there is a big difference between a *church* computer system which has a long term role in the strategy of the church, and a system which, though used for the church is championed by just one person (minister or lay) and would cease to have a role in the church if that person left.

In the study described below, the majority of applications

are used purely for administrative purposes – for tasks that would have been undertaken even in the absence of IT. Very little evidence was found of churches that had gained strategic benefits from IT.

Hence the task of an IT strategy in a church context is to find a means in which the overall mission of the church can be translated into appropriate uses of IT, but taking account of the very low-level of IT investment that is usually possible.

Despite the rapid growth in use of IT in the church sector, there remain many churches with no computer systems at all (at least not under the ownership of the church itself). In many cases the strategy will therefore be concerned with the initial introduction of IT (where required).[8]

A clear need thus exists for a method which could be used in churches to assist the effective introduction of computer-based systems in a manner that will directly support the mission and strategy of the church. (Methodologies to support the analysis, design, and implementation of information systems (IS) have formed a major research theme over the last thirty years[9] – but it was found that none of the existing well-known methodologies is particularly suited to the needs of local churches, or indeed for any kind of small non-profit organisations with limited resources.[10])

3.   I.T. Strategy for Churches

Concepts of IT Strategy

The notions of 'IT strategy' of or 'the strategic use of IT' arise frequently in discussion of information systems (IS), but few authors offer precise definitions. In this discussion, the term is used in the sense of applying IT in a way that will enable an organisation more effectively to fulfil its organisational objectives. It thus follows that the issue of IT strategy can only be examined in relation to mission or strategy of the organisation as a whole.

Strictly speaking, IT strategy is only one aspect of a broader IS strategy, as the latter may well address issues unrelated to technology, although there is a great diversity of ways in which the terms are used.[11] The focus of the present study was upon enabling churches and voluntary organisations to develop strategies to use IT effectively. However, any such strategy manifestly involves extensive consideration of organisational issues; it is not purely related to technology.

Earl,[12] sees this strategic view of IT as emerging around 1980. He distinguishes a 1970s view of IT in terms of *supporting* business strategy (referred to here as the administrative model) from a 1980s model that IT can itself *provide* strategic opportunities (the strategic model). The administrative model of IT is mainly concerned with improving efficiency, whereas the strategic model is concerned with new opportunities. Given that most churches are not primarily administrative organisations, the benefits of IT on the former model are limited, but on the latter model, the potential benefits are huge.

However, a big part of the difficulty in developing an IT strategy is the process of discovering possible ways of using IT which will directly support the overall mission of the church or organisation.

In a large commercial context a wide range of alternative IT developments might be considered for their possible strategic contribution, but it is difficult for churches and small voluntary groups to think in these terms. This is partly due to lack of internal business analysts in small organisations, but more specifically, bespoke software solutions are very unlikely to be possible at a local church level and possible IT solutions thus depend mainly on availability of existing software packages. (This is not to exclude the many cases where individuals have developed one-off IT systems in particular churches, but it is extremely rare for such systems to be documented and supported to the level that they can be reliably used on a long-term basis as strategic systems without the availability of the person who developed them.)

To overcome this difficulty it is proposed here that one major strategic issue for all churches is COMMUNICATION – both within the church (such as from the leadership to the membership as a whole) and from the church as a whole to the community it serves. Indeed many would argue that the communication of the gospel – in appropriate ways for the specific local context – is central to the mission of *any* church. In other words, by focusing on communication as a central area for examining the use of IT, there is a good chance of achieving strategic benefits. In fact, investigations showed that this is an area in which even very small scale use of IT can make a huge difference: for example, by facilitating better presentation and distribution of literature.

Research Method

A three stage programme of fieldwork was employed to investigate these issues. Some initial quantitative data on issues of IT in churches was available from the work of Hardcastle,[13] and the present requirement of devising an IS methodology for this sector demanded extensive considera- tion of cultural and attitudinal issues in the organisations concerned. A qualitative approach was thus adopted, based on detailed case studies with ten churches at different stages of computerisation.

In a first phase, three churches were selected with no church-owned IT at present, to act as a control against which attitudes in the other churches could be assessed. In the second phase four were chosen which had taken explicit decisions to acquire computer systems at least 12 months previously. A final phase involved three further churches which were willing to consider the use or development of IT in the ensuing months, and which were prepared to take part in initial trials of a new approach. A minimum size of around 100 members was set, to ensure the churches would have sufficient complexity to raise reasonable problems of internal communication.

Arising from the first two phases, and drawing on existing literature, a preliminary version of the new IT method was proposed on paper. This was investigated on an action research basis with the three churches in the third phase of studies, and subsequently refined to give the method reported here.

Requirements of an IS Methodology for churches

In order to devise a specific approach or methodology to support the implementation of strategic information systems in a church context, it must meet a number of requirements.

In the first place it must cover the full range of issues from identifying church strategy, to information strategy, to IS planning, IT development, and IT implementation. It is simply not viable with very small systems to have to use a number of separate methodologies. Second, it must be culturally acceptable in the church sector. Thirdly, the actual process by which an IS methodology is applied must recognise the special nature of users in church organisations. The lack of IT professionals means that the users will normally themselves be the implementers of any new systems proposed. They must therefore be able to participate fully in the methodology used. But equally, some of the users will frequently be lay people with no contractual obligation to the church, and their time may be very limited, so for a methodology to be effective, it must be applicable with only a modest time commitment by those concerned.

Finally, an IS methodology for this sector must address longer term issues. IS failures are common even in commercial environments, where employees may be held directly accountable for their performance, but at least project management and reporting techniques are widely available to address such risks. In the non-profit sector such accountability is less frequently applicable, and even where IT solutions are successfully chosen and established initially, the fieldwork reported below found a whole range of reasons why systems can fall into disuse. These include changes of volunteer personal, pressures of other commitments, failure to address practical issues such as data backups, and lack of user pressure to generate results. It follows that for an IS methodology to give strategic benefits in a church, the methodology must itself ensure that the long term success of any new system is at the heart of the process.

Philosophy of the ITEM Approach

The term ITEM originates from the acronym 'Information Technology Ecclesiastical Method' although the approach has subsequently been broadened to indicate its use in a wide range of community organisations, and the term is then generalised to 'Information Technology Environmental

Method' in that it reflects the environment in which voluntary bodies operate.

ITEM is developed to meet the issues identified above. Its philosophy draws heavily on Mumford's socio-technical method known as ETHICS.[14] Nevertheless, ITEM is *not* an attempt to *adapt* ETHICS itself for use in a church context. Rather, it was found that of the main existing IS methodologies, ETHICS appears to come closest in its general philosophy to what is needed for introducing IT in churches, and it can contribute *relevant insights* for the present purpose.

The origins of ETHICS are mainly with large organisations of fulltime staff with many individuals working side by side on similar tasks which are to be organised in a new way using IT. As documented by Hirschheim,[15] ETHICS involves no less than 25 stages *before* getting to any definite implementation proposals, and many of these would require more than one meeting of the design group with investigations in between. A methodology for churches would thus almost certainly have failed if it simply attempted to condense ETHICS into a formula for churches and voluntary groups, as it would be cumbersome, and would still fail to address many of the special issues identified as being crucial to the effective implementation of IT in this sector. Furthermore, ETHICS gives little attention to the implementation stage – which in large organisations would be handled by IT professionals – but which was found to be crucial for any long term success from IT in a church/community context, where the users are very likely to be the implementers.

4.   Description of Item

As finally revised, following the final field studies, ITEM may be outlined as follows. A report is available[16] which is intended as a manual for use by facilitators and others wishing to employ the approach.

The purpose of ITEM is to enable a church or small voluntary organisation to devise, evaluate, and (if agreed) implement an IT strategy that will lead to genuine strategic benefits for the organisation as a whole.

The Project Team and Facilitator

The use of ITEM is based on the interaction between a project team from within the organisation, and an external facilitator; a pattern justified from Mumford's work discussed above.

The facilitator needs not only to have an appreciation of the method, but requires reasonable experience of IT implementation in similar non-commercial organisations in order to provide the education required. However, bearing in mind the limited resources of churches and community organisations and the need to avoid large consultancy costs, the approach is designed to required direct involvement by the facilitator for only four meetings, typically spaced out over a six month period. After that point, ITEM seek to give the project team sufficient autonomy to continue without external involvement.

In order to have the required credibility, the project team should be appointed by the body which has ultimate authority in the church or organisation, typically a church council or church meeting (referred to here as *the council*). The team should comprise between five and seven persons, drawn from a number of roles in the church, including both employees (e.g. minister, parish secretary) and volunteers (lay people with responsibilities). The team should not be filled with computer experts – it is those within the organisation who could most directly benefit from IT whose involvement is crucial – although there should be at least one person who would be willing to act as *computer co-ordinator* if an IT solution is agreed. In a church, for example, the team would typically include the minister, one or two senior lay people, the treasurer, someone concerned with publications, and one or two prospective computer operators.

The term 'users' is to be understood in the broad sense of those directly affected by information processed, not just those who will directly operate any system. It is essential to the method that the users are not involved simply for the purposes of consultation: they are fundamentally in charge of the process, and at the end of the day they make the decisions as to how they wish to proceed – the facilitator only has a supporting role. The project team is directly responsible for making recommendations to the council once it has determined its proposals, and for implementing the system if approval is given.

Structure of the Approach

In order to keep the work manageable, ITEM is structured around five stages, each of which culminates in a meeting of the project team; these are summarised in the Table below.

A major issue in developing the approach was to keep the number of meetings and steps down to a level that would retain the commitment of lay volunteers, whilst providing the team with sufficient opportunity to explore the issues needed to develop a reasonably coherent IT strategy. Churches are well known for creating working parties which make little progress; the structure of ITEM is intended to permit the level of discussion and consultation which is crucial in this sector, but with highly focused actions to be taken at each stage.

The emphasis on communication is a key factor in this. It can be argued that achieving improved internal and external communication is fundamental to the strategy of most organisations, but this is particularly so in churches where much is done by persuasion and where contact has to be maintained with many who may give only a small amount of time to the organisation. By highlighting the issue of communication, the facilitator can enable the team to move from church organisational strategy to IT strategy much more easily than if this had to be done in the abstract.

Stage 1:   *Organisation Strategy and IT Possibilities*

The first stage involves initial contact between the church and the prospective faclitator, as arrangements for the project are established. An initial instigator within the organisation will need to seek approval from the council for the establishment of a project team for this purpose.

Table: Summary of the Stages of ITEM

STAGE	DESCRIPTION	LIKELY DURATION	MAIN MEETING	EDUCATION BY FACILITATOR
Stage 1	Organisation Strategy and IT Possibilities	8 weeks	1st Team Meeting (Full day)	IT Possibilities in Churches
Stage 2	Considering Human Implications of IT	3 weeks	2nd Team Meeting (Half day)	Systems Selection and Types of User
Stage 3	Technical Issues & Formal Proposals	4 weeks	3rd Team Meeting (Full day)	Implementing a Church Computer System
Stage 4	Decision & Implementation	12 weeks	4th Team Meeting (Evening)	*No formal education, but advice given for longer term*
Stage 5	The Long Term Contribution of IT	This stage continues long term	Meetings approx 6-monthly	*(Facilitator has withdrawn-team now in full control)*

Each stage culminates in a main meeting of the project team, which will come at the end of the period indicated. At stage 3, the team decides whether to proceed, and if so, proposals are presented to the council at the start of stage 4. The remainder of the project only proceeds if the team's proposals are approved.

The first meeting of the project team and facilitator will be on an all-day basis (in churches typically on a Saturday). The morning agenda will include: initial introductions; explanation of ITEM, briefing of the facilitator by the team regarding the nature of the church, an initial presentation by the facilitator on IT possibilities in the field concerned, agreement of project boundaries, and appointment of a chair and secretary for the team. Following a working lunch, the team will begin discussions about the strategy of the organisation, will seek to identify consequent ways in which communication could be improved, and will form preliminary views about relevant IT applications, and individuals who would be affected by them.

The facilitator has the task of empowering the team to move from consideration of organisational strategy, to communication, to the beginnings of an IT strategy. Although in large organisations such discussions would take many months, the research suggests that in the context of churches and small community organisations it is realistic to attempt this in a single day.

At the end of the first meeting an action plan is devised, which will mainly involve team members in consulting and interviewing others in the organisation who would be affected by their ideas, with a view to assessing the likely strategic benefits of their suggestions and the human and social implications of doing certain work by computer.

Stage 2: *Considering Human Implications of IT*

About three weeks later a second full meeting takes place (on a half-day basis) where the team review the results of their investigations, and begin to refine their initial suggestions into the beginnings of an IT strategy. Key application areas are selected which can be expected to offer strategic benefits, particularly in terms of improving communication and the facilitator gives a presentation about the principles of systems selection and user responsibilities.

Plans are then set for the technical investigation – in most cases the main issues will be to evaluate appropriate software packages and to locate a suitable hardware supplier. Determination of precise costs is also vital.

Stage 3: *Technical Issues and Formal Proposal*

Following four to five weeks for the technical investigation, the team will convene for a further full day meeting with the facilitator. This third meeting is central to the ITEM approach.

Initially the team will review the results of their investigations, and will agree the precise applications to progress (certain areas may have to be rejected for lack of available or affordable software, for example). The facilitator then encourages the team to set out a number of alternative IT solutions to the needs identified. The solutions could well involve different scales of systems (one machine or several), different patterns of user involvement, different software choices. One of the options may be to avoid IT completely. The team must then evaluate these and agree on their 'best' solution, taking into account the constraints of the church in terms of finance, personnel, etc.

At this stage the facilitator changes the atmosphere and presses the team to stand back and consider their 'best' solution and agree whether, overall, they believe it offers sufficient strategic benefits to justify proceeding. If the decision is 'yes' then the team is committed to proposing this solution to the council and personally implementing it if it is agreed. However, the team must also be completely free to respond 'no' if they do not believe their ideas offer sufficient benefits to justify proceeding. (In the latter case a brief report is presented to the council and the project is wound up.)

If the agreed response is to support the proposal, the team continues, with the facilitator's support, to produce an implementation plan, spelling out precisely what applications will be implemented by what dates, and what benefits can reasonably be expected. The implementation plan is vital to prevent good ideas being endlessly postponed, which is a common problem in a sector that is not motivated primarily by finance. Proper allowance is vital in the plan for training time – the training will often be largely on a self-taught basis, for reasons of cost.

Stage 4: *Decision and Implementation*

The project team now has to produce a short report or presentation for the church council, regarding their proposals. The nature of this report is crucial – it is not just a costed list of items for purchase – but rather it is a proposal of how exactly the team sees IT as contributing to the mission and strategy of the church, including details of dates from the implementation plan when benefits can be expected.

The proposals are presented to the council for a formal

decision to be made. If approval is received, a 'contract' comes into effect between the council and the team, in that the council is agreeing to provide resources and the team is agreeing to deliver results which enhance the mission of the church. The rationale for this is to prevent the tendency for IT plans to drift and for IT usage to lack accountability, which the earlier phases of the research identified as frequent problems in this sector.

If approval is not given, the team has the option of coming up with new proposals or abandoning the project. However, preliminary trials found the nature of the approach makes it unlikely that unrealistic proposals will be put forward by the team, and hence the chances of approval are very good.

Once approval is given, the relevant hardware and software are ordered, and the implementation plan is put into effect in terms of initial setting up and training, and the involvement of the different users agreed. The commitment that team members made as part of the 'contract' with the council is crucial at this stage.

About two months after delivery of the equipment, a fourth full project team meeting takes place, the last involving the facilitator, at which they will review progress against the implementation plan. The format of this meeting forms the basis for subsequent meetings of the team as they continue to review progress on a long term basis (but independently of the facilitator). A extensive checklist agenda is used to ensure that a large number of practical issues have been addressed such as data backups, maintenance arrangements, software support, interrelationships between users, and other factors which were found in the preliminary research to be frequent causes of IT failures in church work. The aim is to prevent the team falling into major problems by picking them up at an early stage.

Stage 5: *The Long Term Contribution of IT*

The final stage of ITEM is the ongoing development of the project (by now the team is self-sufficient and the facilitator is no longer involved).

The team is advised to meet formally at least twice-yearly

to review progress against the implementation plan and to address any new issues that have arisen. Changes of user present a specific issue, if existing users have to leave the organisation or move on to other tasks. Findings from the earlier research indicate that a change of user often leads to initially successful systems falling into disuse. ITEM seeks to address this by keeping responsibility with a team rather than an individual.

A further central aspect of ITEM is that the church council must require the project team, as part of its 'contract', to report back at least annually on the progress that has been achieved, particularly in terms of contribution to the church's mission and strategy. This ensures the council will maintain its 'management commitment' to the project – without this, users can be tempted to give up when difficulties arise.

In due course, the team may go on to propose further development of the use of IT, and the ITEM process can then become iterative over a period of years as new proposals are made.

5.   Effective IT – Theological Issues

Extensive evaluation of the ITEM approach must await further research, but the phase 3 case studies (although based on a preliminary version of ITEM) showed encouraging results. In all three cases, the team's proposals were accepted by their church councils (which is in part an endorsement of the work) and team members went on to put proposals into effect. More significantly, comparing the phase 3 churches with their closest parallels in phase 2 showed that in all three cases the churches using ITEM had achieved much more in a given timescale than the earlier cases. In two of the three cases there was clear evidence of commitment to a strategic role for IT, and even in the third case it was clear that the church would see administrative benefits. It should be noted that the phase 2 churches were selected on the basis that they would be *expected* in the light of earlier research (such as that of Hardcastle[17]) to be reasonably successful in the use of IT, so if those in phase 3 showed further improvement, this could be significant.

How successful the approach is will also depend greatly on the type of organisation, and the commitment of the project team. Even within churches, there were initial indications that higher levels of IT effectiveness are achievable in those churches coming close to Rudge's *systemic* model of church organisation[18] than in churches of other models. But the field trials clearly demonstrated that it is possible, even within organisations as small as local churches, to enable a team to implement IT in relation to the strategic needs of the organisation, rather than just as an administrative resource.

Commitment has been widely documented as crucial to the success of any IT project,[19] and this is as true in churches as in large commercial organisations. The ITEM approach offers a structure in which such commitment may be developed, by relating the use of IT in a 'contract' with the church council or equivalent. However, commitment in a church context can never be reduced purely to questions of organisational arrangements and suitable motivation. It is fundamentally an issue of faith in the gospel and in the mission of the church.

It is thus suggested, in conclusion, that for churches to use IT effectively in ways that directly support their overall mission, those who form part of any project team, or who are involved with IT on a day to day basis, must have a clear perception of the doctrine of the church. They need to be able to feel – almost intuitively – that what they are doing with IT is not merely helping the church to function as an organisation – but is supporting the inauguration of the kingdom of God.

Those who use information technology or information systems of any kind in the work of the church are stewards of information. Over the centuries the Church has taken very seriously its role in the transmission of the gospel, and the words of scripture in particular: indeed the churches were at the forefront of the development of printing. But this stewardship must extend – to a greater or lesser extent – to *all* information entrusted to the church, whether it is the name and address of new contact in the community or financial information about levels of giving. A failure in one of these areas can lead to a failure in the church's mission just as much as a failed sermon in a service of worship.

Thus if churches are to develop strategies for using IT in relation to their mission, methods such as ITEM may help. But there is also a massive need for teaching and reflection on the role of information at local church level, so that IT is not seen as minor practical issue, but as part of the means by which the local church fulfils its primary mission.

NOTES

1. Johnson, G. and Scholes, K., *Exploring Corporate Strategy* 3rd edn. Prentice Hall, 1993.

2. Brierley, P., *Vision Building* Hodder & Stoughton, 1989.
   Bacon, F., Planning Your Church's Programme (Equipping Your Church for Tomorrow – Workbook 1, Bristol & District Association of Baptist Churches, 1987).
   Gibbs, E., I Believe in Church Growth (revised edn), Hodder & Stoughton, 1985).

3. Rudge, P. F., *Ministry and Management* Tavistock, 1968.

4. Rudge, P. F., op. cit. 1968.

5. *Faith in the City*, Report of the Archbishop's Commission on Urban Priority Areas, General Synod of the Church of England, 1985.

6. Marsh, N., *Computers in Voluntary Groups* – Five Case Studies NCVO, 1985.
   Irving, I., *Voluntary Organisations and New Technology* NCVO, 1986.
   Morgan, G. G., *Church Computing: A Strategy* Jay Books, 1987.

7. Berman, F., and Dewhurst, L., *Which Software? Which Hardware?* Inter-Action, 1987.
   Morgan, G. G., op. cit., 1987.

8. Morgan, G. G., 'ITEM: A Strategic Approach to Information Systems in Voluntary Organizations' *Journal of Strategic Information Systems* 4(3) Sep 1995.

9. Wood-Harper, A. T. and Fitzgerald, G., 'A Taxonomy of Current Approaches to Systems Analysis' *The Computer Journal*, 25(10), 12–16, 1982.
   Benyon, D. and Skidmore, S., 'Towards a Took Kit for the Systems Analyst' *The Computer Journal*, 30(1), 2–7, 1987.

10. Morgan, G. G., *The Strategic Use of Information Technology for the Improvement of Communication in Churches* (PhD Thesis, Bristol Polytechnic – now University of the West of England, 1992).

11. Boaden, R. and Lockett, G., 'Information technology, information

220   MANAGEMENT AND MINISTRY

systems and information management: definition and development'
(European Journal of Information Systems 1(1), 23–32, 1991.

12. Earl, M. J. (ed), *Information Management: The Strategic Dimension*
(papers from 1st Annual Oxford PA *Conference on Information Management*) Oxford University Press (p. 4) 1988.

13. Hardcastle, N., *A Survey and Analysis of Effective Computing for Churches* (2 vols) British Council of Churches, 1987.

14. Mumford, E. and Hensall, D., *A participative Approach to Computer Systems Design* Associated Business Press, 1979.

Mumford, E., *Designing Human Systems* Manchester Business School, 1983.

Mumford, E., *'Participative Systems Design'* (The Computer Journal, 27(3), 283, 1984.

Mumford, E. and MacDonald, W. B., *XSEL's Progress: The Continuing Journey of an Expert System* John Wiley pp. 31–37, 1989.

Mumford, E. *Designing Human Systems for Health Care – The ETHICS Method* Eight Associates, 1993.

15. Hirschheim, R. *Office Automation: A Social and Organizational Perspective* John Wiley, 1985.

16. Morgan, G. G., *The ITEM Report* (Faculty of Computer Studies and Maths Report No. CSM 92–1, University of the West of England, Bristol – copies available price £4 from the Faculty Administrator, 1992.

17. Hardcastle, N., op. cit., 1987.

18. Rudge, P. F., op. cit., 1968.

19. Waters, S. J., *Three C's of Successful IT Projects* (Annual International Banking Conference) Institute of Banking, 1986.

Modem's background

ALAN HARPHAM

In 1991 CORAT, the Christian Organisations Research and Advisory Trust, decided with the Bishop of Lambeth, the Rt Revd Ronald Gordon, to call a consultation meeting of all interested parties to review its work over the previous twenty years or so and to determine whether it should continue as an organisation, change direction, launch further initiatives and so on. The consultation was held in the crypt of Lambeth Palace on 4 December 1991, was opened by the Duke of Richmond, President of CORAT, and was chaired by the Rt Revd Christopher Mayfield, Bishop of Wolverhampton (now Bishop of Manchester). The participants came representing only themselves but from a number of backgrounds – churches, church service agencies, universities, business consultancies, charities, theological colleges, voluntary bodies, and business. The meeting was lively and people felt that something important could happen between those who offered expertise and those who recognised that there was something here which could help them.

As a direct result of this meeting the CORAT board called a further meeting on 20 February 1992 at St Peter's Church in Eaton Square, London. The aim of this second meeting was to 'encourage the creation of a (new) network of communication for individuals and organisations who wish to keep in touch with research work and other sources of information relating to the organisational and managerial aspects of the work of Christian bodies'.

Both these meetings generated a lot of excitement and enthusiasts with lively discussion. At the end of the St Peter's meeting a small steering group was constituted to maintain

the considerable sense of momentum that had been established and plan the initial way forward. It took as its working title a suggesting made at the second meeting 'The
Effective Development of ministry using Managerial and
Organisational Disciplines'.

This initial steering group comprised: Dr Geoffrey Ahern
(Management Consultant), Raymond Clarke (Chairman,
treasurer & CORAT Trustee), Alan Harpham (Management
Consultant), John Nelson (Postgraduate researcher & retired
management lecturer), Lawrence Nevard (Leadership
Development Group) and Revd Canon Dr Norman Todd
(Archbishop's Advisor for Bishop's Ministry). The steering
group undertook four tasks:

(a) to produce a straightforward register of those attendees
     who wished to participate and of the services which they
     or their organisations are able to contribute.
(b) to find a suitable publication for articles and informa-
     tion. We started a dialogue with *Ministry* the journal of
     the Edward King Institute, and agreed to use this publi-
     cation as a communication channel rather than launch-
     ing another publication.
(c) to give thought to the status, purpose and structure of a
     more permanent organisation to follow on from the
     work of the steering group encouraging co-operation
     between Christian and secular organisations.
(d) to plan the next full meeting to follow up the two previ-
     ous meetings convened by CORAT.

The next full meeting was held on 25 November 1992 at
Westminster Cathedral in the Archbishop's house. The meeting was very well attended and was chaired by Professor
Jennifer Tann of Birmingham University. The meeting was
presented with a progress report by the steering group,
together with a 'directory of members' for distribution. The
meeting generally welcomed the progress report, but also
identified the need for this to be a two way process based on
a mutuality of learning between church and secular organisations. This was the only change in direction identified by
the attendees. At the end of the meeting volunteers for a

'new' steering group were sought to plan for the formal launch of an organisation – MODEM. In preparing the 'director' we had sought suggestions for a new name. The steering group accepted, at least for the foreseeable future the name – MODEM (Managerial and Organisational Disciplines for the Enhancement of Ministry).

The funding up to the Westminster meeting was provided by voluntary donations from some of the 'members' and a grant from the Christian Initiative Trust. The Christian Initiative Trust continued to provide 'pump priming' funding up to and beyond the formal launch of the charity. Without this funding the organisation would never have been formed.

The 'new' steering group comprised: Peter Bates (European Young Homelessness Network), Peter Brierley (Christian Research Association), Raymond Clarke, (Treasurer and CORAT Trustee), Bob Cumber (AMED – Association of Management Education and Development), Desmond Curry (Sussex Churches Ecumenical Officer), Malcolm Grundy (Avec), Alan Harpham (Chairman), John Nelson, Lawrence Nevard (Leadership Development Group), and Norman Todd (Archbishop's Advisor on Bishop's Ministry).

The steering group agreed to:

- develop a brochure setting out the Purpose, Mission, Vision, Slogan, thrusts and benefits of membership
- draft an outline constitution and organisation structure, and
- plan and run a meeting to launch MODEM

This launch meeting was held in the Council Chamber of the Free Church Federal Council on Tuesday 29 June 1993. MODEM was formally launched at the meeting which was chaired by Revd Canon Martin Reardon (General Secretary of Churches Together in England) and addressed in a keynote talk by Professor Gillian Stamp (Director of the Brunel Institute of Organisational & Social Studies.)

The draft constitution based on establishing MODEM as a charity was accepted by the meeting. Canon Martin Reardon, Professor Gillian Stamp, Raymond Clark and Canon Dr Norman Todd agreed to be the first Trustees. A management committee of ten members to run the day to day affairs of MODEM was elected at the meeting. This included all the members of the previous steering group with the exception of Lawrence Nevard. His place was filled by Hilary Ineson of the Church of England's Board of Education.

MODEM's first two corporate members were the Woolwich Building Society and Church House (Church of England). The Institute of Management subsequently became another corporate member.

In MODEM's first year it:

(a) attracted a membership of over 100.
(b) applied to the Charity Commissioners for registration as a charity.
(c) published a first Directory of Members (1994) – thanks to the Christian Research Association.
(d) contributed articles to *Ministry*, and issued it to all members. *Ministry* is published by the Edward King Institute for Ministry Development.
(e) planned, presented and published summaries of four excellent seminars and workshops, covering:
     – Quality Management and the application of BS5750 (and all that) to the church
     – Leadership – in the church and secular world
     – Regional Structures in ecumenical organisations, and
     – Appraisal schemes
(f) presented a first book review on *The Empty Raincoat* by Charles Handy.
(g) started to plan first MODEM publication – a book tracking the history of management and organisation in ministry and setting the agenda for the subject for the next decade – John Nelson (Secretary) is the Editor of the book.

The first AGM was held at Chelsea Methodist Church on Wednesday 19 October 1994. There were two presentations on 'Why MODEM is important to the churches and the secular world' given by Right Revd Christopher Mayfield, Bishop of Manchester, and Christine Hayhurst of the Institute of Management respectively.

The AGM voted in a New Management Committee, with twelve members and agreed that four should retire by rotation each year:

Peter Bates (Treasurer & European Young Homelessness Network), Peter Brierley (Christian Research Association), Desmond Curry (Sussex Churches' Ecumenical Officer), Steve Dick (Membership Secretary & Secretary of the professional association for Ministers of the General Assembly of Unitarian & Free Christian Churches), Malcolm Grundy (Editor of Ministry), Alan Harpham (Chairman & Co-Chairman of the St Albans and Oxford Ministry Course), Christian Hayhurst (Institute Secretary – Institute of Management), Hilary Ineson (Church of England's Board of Education), John Jordan (Management Consultant & member of the Turnbull Commission), Bernard Kilroy (Senior Lecturer – South Bank University), John Nelson (Secretary & Retired Management Lecturer), and Norman Todd (Archbishop's Advisor on Bishop's Ministry).

In 1995 MODEM:
- obtained charity status with the Charity Commissioners
- further increased its membership to around 150
- ran a further four seminars
  - The Learning Organisation
  - MODEM's Future Status
  - Appropriate Applications of IT to the Churches
  - Public, Business and Voluntary Sectors – How do they Relate?

and planned a further three in 1995 and early 1996, namely:

- The Spirit of the Management of Change
- Ministry in a Secular World
- Ministry in Secular Employment

- Issued its first 'invitations to tenders' on behalf of the Jerusalem Trust to members
- Delivered its first 'members' Handbook

- Advanced its MODEM publication – now with a foreword by Sir John Harvey-Jones and due for publication in 1996
- Had its first letters published in the *Church Times* and the Tablets on the subject of the Turnbull Report

At the 1995 AGM the Rt Revd Chris Mayfield, Bishop of Manchester, agreed to become MODEM's fifth Trustee – an excellent addition. Peter Brierley, Hilary Ineson and John Jordan stood down from the Management Committee. Brian Pettifer (Ministry Deployment Officer/Selection Secretary for the Church of England's Advisory Board of Ministry), Jack Fallow (Company Director) and Harry Speight (Chartered Engineer) were elected in their place.

MODEM aims to achieve its vision:

'That by the year ad 2000 the values and disciplines of those engaged in the mangement of secular and Christian organisations will be mutually recognised and respected.'

If you would like more information on MODEM contact the Editor – John Nelson (also MODEM's Secretary) on 01704-873973

Contributors

Bemrose, Chris *(Chapter 9)*
Mr Chris Bemrose. Currently spending a year with the L'Arche Community in France, a Christian Community which works throughout the world with people with learning difficulties and mental handicaps. Previously a Partner of Compass Partnership, a management consultancy which works exclusively with church and voluntary and not for profit organisations. A member of MODEM.

Brierley, Peter *(Chapter 11)*
Dr Peter Brierley. Executive Director of Christian Research, an independent charity providing publications and seminars on leadership and management for church leaders. Editor of the UK Christian Handbook. A former Civil Service statistician and Programme Director of the Bible Society. Started MARC Europe. A member of MODEM.

Clark, David *(Chapter 4)*
Revd Dr David Blark. Methodist minister and senior lecturer at Westhill College, Birmingham, specialising in community education. Co-ordinator of the Christians in Public Life Programme (CIPL) and its major project – the Human City Initiative focussed on the City of Birmingham. A member of MODEM.

Cross, Hugh *(Chapter 1)*
Revd Hugh Cross. Baptist minister who pioneered a local ecumenical partnership (LEP) in Hemel Hempstead in the 1970s. Ecumenical Officer for England with the British Council of Churches in the 1980s. Recently retired from the post of Ecumenical Moderator for the Milton Keynes Christian Council (1991–1995).

Goldie, David *(Chapter 5–joint)*
Canon David Goldie. Vicar, Christ the Cornerstone, Milton Keynes. Borough Dean. Chairman of the Oxford Diocesan House of Clergy. Member of General Synod. Formerly Curate at Christ Church, Swindon, Mission Priest at Irvine and Priest Missioner at Milton Keynes.

Gonin, Chris *(Chapter 12)*
Revd Chris Gonin. Parish priest in the rural parishes of Milton Ernest and Thurleigh in North Bedfordshire. Formerly a Regional manager for Relate Marriage Guidance. Open University Tutor for course B789. 'Managing

Voluntary and Non Profit Enterprises'. 36 years in the Anglican ministry. Open University MBA in 1992. A member of MODEM.

Greenwood, Robin *(Chapter 8)*
Canon Dr Robin Greenwood. Ministry Development Officer for Chelmsford Diocese. Co-Director of the Edward King Institute. Twenty six years of ordained ministry in the C. of E. in parishes and as a diocesan officer for issues about mission, ministry and spirituality.

Grundy, Malcolm *(Overview and Editorial Advisor)*
The Ven. Malcolm Grundy. Archdeacon of Craven (Bradford Diocese). Founder of the Journal 'Ministry'. Author of books on the relationship between Christianity, work and community. Formerly Senior Chaplain of the Sheffield Industrial Mission, Director of Education and Community for London Diocese, Director of Avec. Member of MODEM's Management Committee.

Harpham, Alan *(MODEM's background)*
Mr Alan Harpham. Group Marketing Director, The Nichols Group (a management consultancy in Project Management). Deputy Chairman of the St Albans and Oxford Ministry Course. Formerly Overseas Contracts Manager with John Laings, Director of Cranfield's MSc Course in Project Management, Churchwarden, Lay Co-Chairman of Elstow Deanery, member of St Alban's Diocesan Synod. Chairman of MODEM's Management Committee.

Harvey-Jones, Sir John *(Foreword)*
Sir John Harvey-Jones MBE. Spent his early years in India but educated in England. Attended the Royal Naval College Dartmouth and served in the Royal Navy. Then joined Imperial Chemical Industries (IC) becoming Chairman from 1982 to 1987. Since he retired has written a number of books and starred in 'The Troubleshooter' Series for BBC TV.

Higginson, Richard *(Chapter 3)*
Dr Richard Higginson. Lecturer in Christian Ethics at Ridley Hall Theological College, Director of the Ridley Hall Foundation which aims to participate in God's mission in the business world through a programme of research, seminars, publications and speaking engagements. Member of MODEM.

Hill, Colin *(Chapter 17)*
Revd Canon Dr Colin Hill. Diocesan Secretary for the Carlisle Diocese. Anglican priest. Canon Residentiary Carlisle Cathedral. Previously Telford Churches' Development Officer for Mission and Ministry, working ecumenically with the Telford Christian Council, and a Rural Dean in the Dioceses of Lichfield and Hereford. Member of MODEM.

Ineson, Hilary *(Chapter 15–joint)*
Ms Hilary Ineson. Advisor in Adult Education and Training of the C of E's Board of Education. Formerly freelance trainer/consultant and Director of Laity Development in Manchester Diocese. Interests include the effects of

unconscious process in groups and institutions, turning adult learning into social action and the training of adult educators, trainers and consultants. Member of MODEM.

Kilroy, Bernard *(Chapter 15–joint and Bibliography–joint)*
Mr Bernard Kilroy. Tutors in management development at South Bank University and the Open University. Former Chief Officer in the social and community housing field in London. Has worked as facilitator to ministry teams with Anglicans, Roman Catholics and Methodists. Member of MODEM's Management Committee.

Morgan, Gareth *(Chapter 19)*
Dr Gareth Morgan. Partner in York-based Kubernesis Partnership which provides advice and training on a range of issues to churches and charities. Also an associate senior lecturer in strategic management at Sheffield Hallam University. Member of MODEM.

Nelson, John *(Editor, Editor's Note, Bibliography–joint, and Index)*
Mr John Nelson. Anglican layman working as a management consultant with the Liverpool Diocese. Formerly Head of Management Studies at Liverpool Polytechnic. Currently engaged in postgraduate research into church leadership. Secretary of MODEM's Management Committee.

Peel, Malcolm *(Chapter 14)*
Mr Malcolm Peel. Formerly Head of Consultancy and Advisory Services with the Institute of Management responsible for accreditation of the Institute under the ISO 9000 quality standard and as Investor in People. Previously held management posts with Rolls-Royce and British Rail. Author of 12 books and 3 published reports on management subjects. Stood for Parliament on three occasions.

Pettifer, Bryan *(Chapter 18)*
Revd Bryan Pettifer. Ministry Deployment Officer/Selection Secretary for the Advisory Board of Ministry of the C of E's General Synod. Previously Principal of the St Albans Diocesan Training Scheme and Residentiary Canon of St Albans Cathedral. Deputy Chairman of MODEM's Management Committee.

Rampton, Val *(Chapter 13–part)*
Revd Val Rampton. Priest in Charge of Kneesall, Laxton and Wellow. Advisor for Women's Ministry in Southwell Diocese. Entered parish ministry in 1980. Previously Lecturer in Geography at Nottingham Trent Polytechnic and Mary Ward College, Keyworth.

Ryan Catherine *(Chapter 7)*
Sister Catherine Ryan. A Roman Catholic religious sister. Lives in community in East London. Holds an MA in Organisational Analysis and Behaviour from Lancaster University where she is researching a PhD. Works in group facilitation and consultancy both within the Eastern Pastoral Area of the RC Diocese of Westminster, and as a freelance. Member of MODEM.

Seeley, Martin *(Chapter 16)*
Revd Martin Seeley. Vicar of The Isle of Dogs, London. Formerly Secretary for Continuing Ministerial Education (CME) for the Church of England's Advisory Board of Ministry.

Stacey, Nicolas *(Chapter 10)*
Revd Nicolas Stacey. Chairman of East Thames Housing Group. Former naval officer and international athlete; Assistant Curate St Marks Portsea, Domestic Chaplain to Bishop of Birmingham, Rector of Woolwich, Dean of London Borough of Greenwich, Six Preacher – Canterbury Cathedral; Deputy Director of Oxfam; Director of Social Services for the London Borough of Ealing and Kent County Council. Member of MODEM.

Stamp, Gillian *(Chapter 2–joint)*
Professor Gillian Stamp PhD. Director of the Brunel Institute of Organisation of Social Studies (BIOSS). Worked with the C of E on issues arising from synodical government, with the Revd Canon Dr Norman Todd in workshops for recently consecrated bishops, with the Reformed Rabbinate and with the Methodists. member of Council of St George's House, Windsor. Trustee of MODEM.

Todd, Norman *(Chapters 2–joint and 6)*
Revd Canon Dr Norman Todd. Anglican priest now freelance consultant in spirituality, psychotheraphy and ministry. Experience in parish ministry and the diocesan level adult education. Until 1995 Archbishop's Advisor for Bishops' Ministry. Graduate in science and theology, a doctorate in psychology, Associate member of BIOSS. Trustee and member of the management committee of MODEM.

Walker, John *(Chapter 13)*
Revd John Walker. Vicar of St John the Evangelist, Carington, Notts. Chair of QIM in the Southwell Diocese. Co-Founder with Revd Canon Dr Norman Todd) of the Quality Initiative as applied to the church's ministry. Ordained 18 years, most of which spent in urban inner-city ministry. Member of MODEM.

Welch, Elizabeth *(Chapter 5–joint)*
Revd Elizabeth Welch. Provincial Moderator for the West Midlands Province of the URC. Member of Central Committee of World Council of Churches. Grew up in South Africa. Ordained to URC ministry and served at the ecumenical Church of Christ the Cornerstone, Milton Keynes 1983–1996. Member of MODEM.

Wilcox, Haydon *(Chapter 13–part)*
Revd Haydon Wilcox. Rector of Bilsthorpe, Newark, Notts. Prior to Ordination worked in retail management. Served in the Church of England for 14 years as a parish priest with experience in urban, mining and rural communities specialising in counselling, adult education, consultancy and community development. Member of MODEM.

Short Bibliography

BERNARD KILROY *and*
JOHN NELSON

Inevitably, any choice means hard decisions about leaving out so many excellent books. This short bibliography was intended as a core list of two dozen titles spread widely over the field, and is already more.

Archbishops' Conference on the Organisation of the Church of England: *Working as One Body*: 1995, Church House Publishing – the Turnbull Commission's recommendations for the central structures (only!).

(RC) Bishops Conference of England & Wales: *The Sign We Give*: 1995, Matthew James – landmark exploration of the principles of collaborative ministry (alas, no case studies).

Brierley, Peter: *Vision Building: Knowing Where You Are Going*: 1989, Hodder & Stoughton – regularly used in its seminars by the Christian Research Association.

Campbell, Alistair V: *Moderated Love: A Theology of Professional Care*: 1984, SPCK – a profound integration of two worlds of ministry.

Capra, Fritjof: *The Turning Point: Science, Society and the Rising Culture*: 1982, Flamingo – a (slightly breathless) doorway to post modern thinking.

Carnall, Colin: *Managing Change: Self Development for Managers*: 1991, Routledge – practical insights for organisations (and self testing) by a Henley prof.

Cowell, Donald: *The Marketing of Services*: 1984, Heinemann – a standard college text, with gimmicks and gismos.

Craig, Yvonne: *Learning for Life*: 1994, Mowbrays – principles of continuous development by a Church House staff facilitator.

Cranwell-Ward, Jane: *Thriving on Stress*: 1990, Routledge – so it's not all negative and can be understood and tamed, maybe (from Henley).

Downs, Thomas: *The Parish as Learning Community*: 1979, Paulist Press NY – optimistic, inclusive and reflective (if only it was as simple as this!).

Drucker, Peter: *Managing the Non-Profit Organisation*: 1990, Butterworth-Heinemann – the guru grandfather of modern management from the USA.

Dulles, Avery: *Models of the Church* (3rd edit): 1995, Gill &Macmillan – straight, broad and sound Jesuit thoughtfulness, if a little too schematic.

Eastell, Kevin (Ed): *Appointed for Growth*: A Handbook for Ministry *Development and Appraisal*: 1994, Mowbray – a stimulating anthology of theory and practice.

Finney, John: *Church on the Move: Leadership for Mission*: 1992, Darton, Longman & Todd – another pastoral primer, which at least asks the basic questions.

Greenwood, Robin: *Transforming Priesthood*: 1995, SPCK – widely regarded as the theological book of the year in 1995.

Grundy, Malcolm: *An Unholy Conspiracy*: 1992, The Canterbury Press Norwich – so ministry and management are not chalk and cheese!

Handy, Charles: *Understanding Voluntary Organisations*: 1988, Penguin – this prolific prof's primer of 'soft' management, brief and brilliant.

Henry, Jane (Ed): *Creative Management*: 1991, Open University/Sage – an anthology of readings for the OU's course in 'creative management'.

Higginson, Richard: *Transforming Leadership: A Christian Approach to Management*: 1996, SPCK – examines how biblical Christianity can contribute to the world of management.

Honey, Peter: *Improve Your People Skills*: 1988, Institute of Personal Management – an A to Z pocket guide, not just a memory jogger.

Johnson, Gerry and Scholes, Kevan: *Exploring Corporate Strategy (Texts and cases)*: 1993, Prentice Hall (3rd Edit) – a standard college text, solid and imaginative, so long as you read the edition with case studies of big business.

Kaldor, Peter and Powell, Ruth: *Views from the Pews: Australian Church Attenders Speak Out*: 1995, Openbook, Adelaide (or United Church Board of Mission) – eye-opening summaries of the National Church Life Survey.

Keirsey, David and Bates, Marilyn: *Please Understand Me; Character and Temperament Types*: 1984, Oxford Psychological Press – maybe the best introduction to Myers Briggs and all that, complete with questionnaire.

Lovell, George: *Analysis and Design: A Handbook for Practitioners and Consultants in Church and Community Work*: 1994, Burns & Oates – the Avec method which in due course will be as Montessori has been to the learning process – a must.

Lyons, Edna: *Partnership in Parish: A Vision for Parish Life, Mission and Ministry*: 1987, Columba Press – a gem from the best Irish RC thinking and practice.

Minear, Paul: *Images of the Church in the New Testament*: 1961, Lutterworth Press – the theological foundation for Peter Rudge, and complements Dulles (above).

Morgan, Gareth: *Images of Organisation*: Beverley Hills, California/Sage – a stroboscopic portrait of organisations, whether as machines, organisms or psychic prisons.

Neibuhr, H. Richard: *Christ and Culture*: 1956, Harper – thorough tour de force from the US protestant tradition, so durable but as hard as oak.

Parkinson, C. Northcote: *Parkinson's Law or the Pursuit of Progress* (illustrated by Osbert Lancaster): 1957, John Murray (and later Penguin) – yes, the endlessly quoted and as piquant and outrageous as horseradish on blancmange.

Pedler, Miek, *et al*: *The Learning Company* – a more practical UK guide than the better known, more profound classics of senge.

Pugh, Derek S. and Hickson, D. J.: *Writers on Organisation* (4th Edition): 1989, Penguin – an anthology from the clockwatchers of the 1920s to the visionaries of the 1960s, and still being added to.

Rudge, Peter F.: *Ministry and Management*: 1968, Tavistock (out of print) – a landmark study of the theological concepts which repays the hard digging required.

Schumacher, E. F.: *Small is Beautiful: A Study of Economics as if People Mattered*: 1974, Abacus – a seminal work which also challenged the impersonal pyramids of classical management.

Senge, Peter M. *et al*: *The Fifth Discipline Fieldbook*. 1994, Nicholas Brealey – what US executives are meant to read on transatlantic flights for rethinking into learning organisations (see Pedler above).

Sofield, L. and Juliano, C.: *Collaborative Ministry: Skills and Guidelines*: 1987, Ave Maria Press, Notre dame, Indiana – a good beginners' guide on working with parish teams from an RC 'brother' and 'sister'.

Stoner, James A. F.: Freeman, R. E. and Gilbert, D. R.: *Management*: 1995, Prentice Hall (6th Edition) – standard college text jam packed with case studies of US management and all too detailed, but there when you want it.

Tiller, J. and Birchall, M.: *The Gospel Community and its Leadership*: 1987, Marshall Pickering – flavour of the C of E evangelical but practical fervour, and why not?

Torrington, Derek and Hall, Laura: *Personnel Management*: 1995, Prentice Hall (3rd Edition) – standard college text, thorough and authoritative.

Widdecombe, Catherine: 'Group Meetings that Work': 1994, St Pauls – builds on the Avec experience and very practical, though ideally complemented by Keirsley & Bates, and Schofield & Juliano (above).

Index

Advisory Board of Ministry (ABM, C of E, 178, 179, 183, 184
Adult learning, 13–15
Affirming Lay Ministries, 59–65
AMED, 223
Anglican, 4, 6, 12, 31, 34, 73, 74, 75, 76, 77, 96, 101, 105, 135, 138, 160, 161, 177, 188, 195, 203
Appraisal, 23, 24, 89, 138, 156, 158, 171–175, 177–185, 191, 193, 224
Appraisal schemes, 177–185
Appropriate professional support and development, 155–169
Archbishop 26, 44, 194, 222
Archdeacons, 100, 102, 179, 196
Asking 'Why' questions now?, 171–175
Avec, 165

Bank of England, 120
Baptism with a Documented Management System (DMS), 142, 143
Baptist Church, 6, 73, 156
Bedfordshire Training and Enterprise Council, 133, 134
Berry, Tony, Dr, 178
Biblical references, 4, 7, 8, 25, 35, 38, 43, 44, 59, 61, 62, 63, 69, 79, 86, 89, 95, 100, 106, 111, 112, 116, 127, 129–131, 135, 137, 145, 192, 196
(see also Jesus references)
Bilthorpe, St Margaret's, Parish Church, Southwell Diocese, 142
Bishops, 8, 19, 20, 22, 31, 32, 34, 35, 44, 48, 49, 51, 54, 77, 91, 100, 101, 102, 111, 116, 122, 123, 124, 138, 156, 162, 172, 174, 179, 196, 221, 224, 225

Black majority churches, 156
Bridgebuilding, bridgebuilders, (leadership images), 8, 9, 20, 26
British Council of Churches, 18
British Social Attitudes Survey, 167
Brunel Institute of Organisational & Social Studies, 223
BS (British Standard) 5750, 24, 141, 142, 152, 153, 166, 224
Budget of opportunities, 20–26

Calling (see vocation)
Cardinal Heenan, 8
Cardinal Hume, 18
Carpenter, Harry, Bishop, 32
Chancellor of the Exchequer, 122
Change, management of, 19, 25, 40, 139
Chairman (Methodist District), 8, 22
Charity Commissioners, 224, 225
Chelsea Methodist Church, 224
Christian Initiative Trust, 223
Christian leaders, 125, 130
Christian parodies of management, 27
Christian Research Association, 223, 224, 225
Christians in Public Life Programme, (CIPL), 67, 69, 71
Church, espec. 111–118, 119–124
– and charities, 112
– and computer systems, 205, 206, 208
– as safe haven, 6
– doctrine (and IT), 218
– government, 77
– management, 111, 116, 117, 171
– particularities, 179
– plants, 15
– structures, 13
– training and learning culture, 6, 7
– values, value system, 136, 192
Church Commissioners, 133

Church of Christ The Cornerstone, Milton Keynes, 73, 75
Church of England, 14, 15, 21, 34, 73, 76, 100, 101, 119–124, 158, 172, 174, 175, 178, 183, 187, 190, 192, 193, 194, 196, 197, 224, 225
– Board of Education, 14
– Revival of, 119–124
Church House, 224
Church leaders, espec. 7–11, 31–36
– as a focus of unity, 8
– as bridge builders, 8, 9, 20, 26
– as shepherds, 7, 8, 20, 38, 48, 49, 96
– nation's expectations of, 197
Church Times, 226
Church Urban Fund, 17

Churches as places of learning, 133–139

Churches, espec. 133–139
– and IT, 201–219, 225
– as hierarchies and bureaucracies – impact on clergy, 93–95
– as instruments of God's own mission, 102
– as learning organisations, 23, 105, 133–139, 167
– as mysteries, 99
– as voluntary non-profit organisations, 26, 111–118, 136
– the management of, 26
Churches Together in England (CTE), 18, 223
Churchmanship, 197
Circuit (Methodist), 12, 22, 26, 35
– Superintendents, (Methodist), 22, 26
Citizen's Charters, 148, 152
Clergy, espec. 99–108, 155–169, 171–175
– and 'a career', 34, 102
– and professionalism, 102
– appraisal and review, 23, 24, 138, 156, 158, 171–75, 177–185, 191
– as leaders and managers, 108
– as people of vision, 107
– breakdown, 156
– career development, 24
– conditions of service, 188, 193, 194
– professional support and development, 155–169
– management role, 196
– (changing) role, 10, 92, 99–108, 195, 196

– self-appraisal, 156
– teams and groups, 26
– training, 26, 50, 195, 198
– using hierarchical, pyramidal method of managing congregations, 14
– vocational/calling, 6, 7
Clericalism, 25, 67, 93, 94, 95, 101, 106, 166
Collaborative learning, 164
Collaborative (shared) ministry, 10, 16, 17, 21, 26, 33, 35, 62, 106, 107, 141, 145, 146, 160, 161, 164
Committees, 16, 18, 113, 114, 115, 117
Communication, 207, 212, 214
Community development, 16, 17
Computer experts, 211
– personal, 204
– systems (and churches), 128, 181, 205, 206, 208
Congregational Church, 31
Continuing ministerial education, 138, 195, 198

Contributors, 227–230

CORAT, 221, 222
Council of Churches for Britain and Ireland (CCBI), 18
Curé d'Ars, 9, 10, 12, 20, 96

Dangers in lay ministry, 59, 60
Dean – Borough, 121
– Cathedral, 122
– Rural, 179
Deanery, 35

Developing a reflective spirituality in management, 83–89

Diaconate (permanent), 25
Diocese(s), 5, 17, 24, 91, 93, 94, 95, 96, 115, 138, 141, 156, 166, 167, 172, 173, 174, 183, 197, 198
– London, 5
– St Albans, 138
– Southwell, 24, 141
– Westminster (RC), 91
Distance Learning, 165
District (Methodist, URC), 17, 24, 35
Documented Management System (DMS), 142–146
– applied to baptism, 142, 143
– applied to leaving a parish, 144, 145
Duke of Rutland, 221
Dunkirk, 126

Ecclesiastical culture, 11, 21
– structures, 10
Ecclesiology, 7, 106
Ecumenical, espec. 17–19, 31–36, 73–81
– activity, 14, 19, 81
– agencies, 18
– Areas of Ecumenical Experiment, 31
– international debate, 101
– Local Ecumenical Partnerships, 73
– Local Ecumenical Projects, 31, 34
– management of, 26
– Moderator (of Milton Keynes), 31–36
– Moderator-in-Council (of Milton Keynes), 33
– organisations, 177
– partnerships, 17, 75
– sensitivities, 76
– staff college, 21
– structures and restructuring, 17, 18, 19, 26, 31–36, 224
– theology, 106
Edward King Institute for Ministry Development, 224
Employment of lay people, 17, 18
Enterprise (and wealth creation), 24, 25
Episcopal, 32, 33, 34, 156, 196
ETHICS, 210
Ethics of business, 24

Faith and work, 61
Faith in the City Report, 203
Free Church(es), 6, 73, 76, 77, 121
Free Churches Federal Council, 223
Freehold, 193, 194

Gender (mixed parishes), 21–22, 73–81
General Synod (C of E), 172, 175
Get up and go, 125–132
God on Monday project, 6
Golf, 126
Gordon, Ronald, Bishop, 221
Governance and management, 115

Haggai Institute for Advanced Leadership Training, 125
Handy, Charles, 23, 224
Hardacre, Canon Ian, 158
Harvey-Jones, Sir John, v, 226
Heenan, Cardinal, 8
Holy management, 102
Home Secretary, 122
Hostility to management, 3–7, 111
House of Bishops (C of E), 172, 194

House of Commons, 99
How to revive the Church, 119–124
HRM (see Human Resource Management)
Hugel von F, 45, 46, 48
Human resource management, 187–199
– a new paradigm of ministry?, 194–196, 198
– and theology, 190–192
– as normative model of personnel management, 187–190
– the management of, 192–194
Hume, Basil, Cardinal, 18
Hunter, Leslie, Bishop, 19

Industrial Mission, 24
Information Systems (IS), 47, 48, 206, 208–210
Information Technology in church mission and strategy, 201–220
Inherited concepts of leadership, 31–36
Institute of Management, 224, 225
Intermediate (ecumenical bodies), 18
International Standards Organisation (ISO) 1986, 147
Internet, 205
'Investors in people', 166, 181
ISO (International Standards Organisation) 9000, 50, 141, 142, 153, 166
ISO (International Standards Organisation) 9000, 9004, 153
IT and theology, 217–219
ITEM, 209–219

Jerusalem Trust, 225
Jesuit, 10
Jesus, 7, 10, 35, 38, 43, 49, 61, 63, 64, 89, 102, 103, 106, 111, 127, 135, 136, 198
Journal of Strategic Information Systems, 201
Journal (Jesuit) 'Human Development', 10

Laity in the RC Church, 13
Lambeth Palace, 221
Lay The, espec. 59–65, 67–71
– affirmation and support, 25, 59–65
– and IT, 209
– church role, 25

– dependence, 14
– development, 25
– employment, 17, 18
– lay training and support, 12, 193
– ministry, 59–65, 67–71
– responsibilities, 12
– vocation, 67–71
Lay Chair (of Milton Keynes
   Ecumenical Council, Executive,
   Assembly), 33
Lay Eucharistic Council, Liverpool,
   1980, 13
Leadership (church) espec. 7–11,
   20–22, 31–36, 79, 92–93, 115–117
– and communication, 207
– and management, 7, 8, 10, 11, 26,
      108, 111, 113, 115–117
– and ministry, 196
– and revival, 23
– and vision, 129
– Christian, 125, 130
– church, 31, 119
– clerical/clergy, 103, 195
– concepts, 20, 159
– cultural, 197
– defined, 92, 93
– denominational, 34
– ecumenical, 18, 31, 32
– effective, 159
– good, 108
– Haggai Institute for Advanced
      Leadership Training, 125
– in collaborative/shared ministry,
      33, 34, 155
– in learning organisations, 11,
      134
– in society, 9, 25, 224
– inherited concepts of, 31–36
– initial and in-service training for,
      21
– local, 34, 102
– mixed gender, 21, 22, 75, 79
– new kind, 36
– no one ideal style, 116
– opportunities, 23
– personal, 33
– professional support for, 26
– quality – principles of, 125
– responsibilities, 18
– role, 92, 130
– servant, 64
– selection of, 9, 10, 21
– team, 106–7
– vacuum, 16

Leadership Development Group, 222,
   223

Learning Organisations, 11, 22–23,
   133–139
– managed ministers as part of, 137,
      138, 139
– planning congregation as part of,
      136, 137
Leaving a parish – the use of a
   Documented Management System,
   143, 144, 145
Legitimacy of business, 63
Lessons from voluntary sector for the
   church, 113
Liberation theology, 165
Life cycle of congregations, 23
Lincoln (cathedral), 139
Liverpool, 13, 67, 156
London Business School, 47
London Diocese, 5
Lund dictum, 32

Managed minister as part of the
   learning organisation, 137, 138, 139
Management (managing, managed)
   espec. 3–27, 83–89, 99–108,
   111–118, 187–199
– activity based, 21
– and business studies, 37
– and governance, 115
– and leadership, 7, 8, 10, 11, 26,
      108, 111, 113, 115–117
– and IT, 47
– and ministry, v, 26, 49, 196
– and oversight (episcope), 196
– and pressures, 64
– and professions, 159–160
– and teamwork, 160
– and the dangers of measurement,
      49, 50
– and theology, 139
– appointments to, 116
– appropriateness
      – for church leaders, 4
      – for inspired amateurism?, 3
– as a concept, concepts of, 6, 115
– as a discipline, 7, 21
– as a science, 7–11, 26
– as an art and not a science, 136
– as an intergrated system, 22
– being left behind, 6
– being managed – bad experiences
      of, 6
– better – the ubiquitous need for, v
– blending – with technical skills, 116
      – the spiritual, 116
– by committee, 16
– by clergy, 196
– characteristics of, 112

– churches need to be, v
– classical, 161
– commitment, 217
– compatibility with informal,
   voluntary congregations?, 3
– consultants, 89
– definition of, 10, 11, 160
– development and battle scars, 4–7
– education, 160
– effective, 4, 83, 84
   and well understood practices as
   pastoral, 4
– everyone is a manager of
   something, 83
– fashions, 105
– historic understandings from Bible
   and church traditions, 4
– Holy, 102
– implicit understandings already
   being practised, 3
– in multiple charge (clergy)
   appointments, 11–12
– in the market place of values, 25
– in voluntary sector, 111
– information as primary currency
   of, 47
– lessons in, 113
– literature, 94
– modern theories, manifestations of,
   11–15, 63–64, 106, 107
– need for responsible management
   in our churches, 19
– new styles, 11
– not primary task for most clergy, 3
– objections, resistance, hostility, to,
   3–7
– of change, 3, 4, 19, 25, 107, 159,
   194, 195
– of charitable, voluntary
   organisations like churches, 11
– of church planting, 15
– of churches as voluntary non-profit
   organisations, 26
– of ecumenism and ecumenical
   structures, 26
– of decline, 23
– of divided churches, 22
– of growth and development, 15
– of large numbers of lay people, 17,
   18
– of organisations, 85
– of teams and groups, (C of E),
   15–16
– of the escape from clericalism, 25
– of time, 5, 107
– of, with, people, 105, 164, 187,
   193

– of the work environment, 159
– opportunities for, 8
– paradies of, 27
– performance disciplines, 49
– poor, 116
– quality, 166
– reflective practice in, 25
– requirements of good, 116
– secular, 167
– seen (and practised) negatively,
   115, 116
– sound – relevant to the churches, v
– strategic, 202
– style, 191, 196
– the corporate culture, 191, 192
– tasks, 10
– theology, 164, 171
– the need for the development of a
   new science of the theologically
   resourced practice of, 26
– training in, 15, 21, 116
– training task, 15
– using the hierarchical, pyramidac,
   method, 14
– with volunteers, 155

Management Charter Initiative, 166
Managerialism, 111
Mayfield, Christopher, Bishop, 221,
   224, 225
Measurement and analysis of faith
   activity, 167
Methodist church, 12, 17, 24, 31, 35,
   73, 74, 76, 121, 156, 224
– District Chairman, 8, 22
Milton Keynes, 18, 31, 32, 33, 34,
   73
Milton Keynes Christian Council, 32,
   33, 34, 73
Ministerial review (see appraisal and
   review)
Ministry, espec. 91–98, 99–108,
   141–146, 155–169, 194–196
– a much more managed, 138
– a new strategy for, 195
– and Baptism and Eucharist – WCC
   Document, 36
– and leadership, 196
– and management, v, 26, 49
– and mission, 160
– activities and tasks of, 164
– appraisal, 156
– as a transaction, 168
– based on the sayings of others, 5
– change in role of, 196
– changing concepts of, 160
– church, 141

– collaborative and shared, 16, 17, 21, 26, 33, 35, 62, 141, 145, 146, 161
– consultant, 51
– continuous development in, 160
– contribution of the lay to, 195
– dangers in lay, 59, 60
– definition of, 164
– definition of management within, 160
– developing, development of, 74, 158
– disciplines of, 50
– Edward King Institute for Development of, 224
– effectiveness of, 163, 167–8
– emphasis in, 163, 167
– enhancements of, 50
– formation, 160
– genuine, 60
– growth of, 166
– in a secular world/secular employment, 225
– in debt counselling, 130
– in its professional context, 156
– lay, 59–65, 67–71
– limited to bishops, priests, deacons, 100
– local, 165
– management of change in, 195
– ministers accountable and responsible directly for, 138
– new developments in, 22
– new paradigm of, 187, 194–8
– non-stipendiary, 123–4
– of the Ecumenical Moderator of Milton Keynes, 35
– opportunity for, 60
– ordained, 11, 36, 95, 108, 171
– organisational dimension of, 165
– pastoral, 96
– personal, 22
– 'presence' of ministry, 165
– process of, 165
– 'professional' dimension of, 168
– purposes, 164
– quality, 141–6
– research needed into, 56
– responsibilities of, 196
– review process, 156
– resources for, 165
– role of, 91–98
     women in 73
– second and third phase, 51, 52
– sparsity of mature, 51
– specialist, 96
– support in, 184

– system of professional development for, 163
– Team and Group in the C of E, 15
– team (mixed gender), 74
– the management of change in, 195
– the skills of, 9
– theological reconstructions of, 13
– theology of, 16
– tradition of ordaining women to, 73
– training for, to a mature laity, 26
– understandings of in the world and the church, 13
– unclear boundaries in, 160
– understanding new patterns of management in, 99–108
– 'professional' dimension of, 168

Ministry, Journal of the Edward King Institute for Ministry Development, 178, 179, 222, 224
Mission statement, 137, 180, 181, 192, 202
Mixed gender teams, 73–83
– decision-making, 78–79
– leadership, 79
– personality v gender, 80
MODEM, iii, v, 3, 11, 18, 37, 57, 64, 178, 201, 221–225
Moderator (URC), 8, 22, 33
Multiple charge (clergy) appointments, 11–12
Myers-Briggs Indicator Workshops, 80

National Council for Vocational qualifications (NCVQ), 166
National Pastoral Congress of the RC Church Liverpool 1880, 67
National Health Service, 179
National Trust, 99
Non-profit organisations (sector), 112, 113, 136, 202, 209
Non-StipendiaryMinistry – NSMs – (C of E), 25, 96, 120, 122, 123, 124
Nottinghamshire, 142

Open College, 165
Open University, 165
Organisational, espec. 15–17, 180–184, 202–206
– issues, 15–17
– core values, 197
– development (and appraisal), 180–184
– mission, 202
– objectives, 202, 206

– skills, 107
– strategy, 202, 203
Overview, 3–27
Oxfam, 122, 159

Paradigm (new, changing) of ministry, 187, 194–196
Parish, 3, 22, 34, 51, 73, 92, 101, 105, 115, 119, 124, 133, 142, 144, 145, 165, 167, 172, 203
– audit, 101, 167, 203
– Woolwich, 121
Parish and People Movement, 13
Partnership (see lay vocation), 68–69
Pastoral President, 32, 33
Pastoral theology, 37, 51
Pastoral theology re-defined, 37–58
Patterns of management in ministry, 99–108
Pentecostal Church, 6
People-in-relationships (P-in-R), 38, 40, 41, 48, 57
People-in-working relationships (P-in-WR), 43, 44, 45, 46, 48, 49, 53, 54, 55
Personal computers, 204
Personhood, 69–70
Personnel management – history of, 187–188
Planning congregation as part of a learning organisation, 136–137
Presbyterian Church (of England), 31
President (Presidency) of the Milton Keynes Ecumenical Council, 33, 34
Priesthood, 6, 13, 25, 96
– as craft, 96
– as profession, 96
– of the laity, 13
– ministerial, 6, 96
Professional support and development (for clergy), 26, 155–169
Professionalism (and clergy), 102
Professions, the, 25, 159, 160
Profit making organisations, 136
Project management, 209
Profit (and profitability) 24, 192, 197, 202
Protestant, 77, 135

Quakers, 68
Quality at work, 147–154
Quality, 24, 141–146, 147–154, 166, 224
– at work, 147–154, 166

– circles, 148, 150
– management, 166, 224
– ministry, 141–146
Quality ministry, 141–146
Quality standards, 24, 141, 142, 153, 166
– BS (British Standard) 5750, 24, 141, 142, 152, 153, 166, 224
– ISO (International Standards Organisation) 9000, 141, 142, 166
– ISO (International Standards Organisation) 9000–9004, 153

Ramsey, Ian, Bishop, 44
Ramsey, Michael, Archbishop, 44, 50
Reardon, Canon Martin, General Secretary of CTE, 223
Reclaiming vocation for the whole people of God, 67–71
Reflective practice in management, 25
Reflective spirituality in management, 83–89
Relationships in mixed gender parishes, 73–81
Revival of the Church of England, 119–124
Ridley Hall Foundation, 63
'Right First Time', 150, 151
Riva management consultants, 141
Roehampton Institute London, 96
Role of clergy (see Clergy role)
Role of ministry, 91–98
Roman Catholic Church, 6, 12, 13, 18, 67, 73, 74, 76, 77, 91, 96, 135, 156, 160
Rotherham, 5
Royal Society of Arts, 47
Rudge, Peter, 14, 164, 203, 218
Rural Deans, 179

St Albans Diocese, 138
St George's House, Windsor, 172
St Peter's Church, Eaton Square, London, 221
Salvation Army, 6
Science of management, 7–11
Science of theologically resourced church management, 26
Selection (of leaders), 9, 10, 21, 161
Shared ministry (see Collaborative ministry)
Shepherd (leadership image), 7, 8, 20, 38, 48, 49, 96

Sheppard, David, Bishop, 156
Short Bibliography, 231–233
Sigmoid Curve, 23, 135
Southwell Diocese, 24, 141
Spirituality, 83–89
  – corporate spirituality in teams,
    88
Standards of quality, 24
Stewards (Stewardship) of
  information, 201, 218
  – of resources, 164
Strategic planning, 93, 113, 114
Support in Ministry (See Appraisal and
  review), 184
Swanwick Declaration 1987, 18
Sweesner, Thomas, 10
Swindon, 31
Swindon Report, 33
Synodical government (review of),
  194

Tablet, The, 226
Tann, Jennifer, Professor, 222
Team and group management, 15–16
Team and group ministry, (C of E), 15,
  16, 26, 35, 74, 102, 106, 107, 122,
  128, 164
Team(s), 22, 73–81, 106, 128
  – leader(s), 128
  – learning, 23, 106
  – Rector, 22
  – mixed gender parish, 73–81
Teamwork and information sharing,
  48
  – and training, 48
Temple, Freddie, Bishop, 31
Thamesdown, 32, 33
Thatcher, Margaret, 126
**The church as a voluntary non-
  profit organisation**, 111–118
Theology, 13, 16, 63, 139, 199,
  217–219
  – and management, 139
  – and IT, 217–219
  – of the laity, 13
  – of ministry, 16
  – of work, 63
  – practical, 199
Time management, 5, 107

Total Quality Management (TQM),
  148, 151
**Towards re-defining the role of
  ministry**, 91–98
Training and Enterprise Councils, 166
  – Bedfordshire TEC, 133, 134
Training in ministry (for clergy), for a
  mature laity, 26
Training in management, 21
Tripod of Work, 42
TUC, 99
Turnbull Commission Report (C of E),
  21, 104, 194, 226

**Understanding new patterns of
  management in ministry**, 99–108

UK Christian Handbook, 128
Unitarian and Free Christian Churches,
  225
United Reform Church (URC), 12, 31,
  73, 75, 156
  – Moderator, 8
University, 57

Vatican Council, 12, 13, 106
Vision, 92, 105–106, 129–131
Vocation/calling, 6, 68–71
  – as a call to partnership, 68–69
  – as a call to personhood, 69–70
  – Christian, 67, 68
  – lay, 68–71
  – of the ordained, 6, 70–71
Voluntary organisations/sector, 111,
  114, 115, 116, 206, 207

Wealth creation and enterprise, 24
Westminster Abbey, 122
Westminster Cathedral (RC), 8, 222,
  223
  – Diocese (RC), 9
Winston Churchill, 131
Women priests, bishops,
  church leaders, 21, 22, 25
Woolwich (Parish), 121
Woolwich Building Society, 224
World Council of Churches, 36, 67
Work seen as a necessary evil, 60
Work consultancy, 158
Worker priests (RC), 96